Street by Street

C000295113

WORT~~~~

ARUNDEL, LITTLEHAMPTON, PULBOROUGH

Amberley, Angmering, Ashington, East Preston, Ferring, Findon, Henfield, Lancing, Rustington, Sompting, Steyning, Storrington, Upper Beeding, West Chiltington Common

1st edition November 2002

© Automobile Association Developments Limited 2002

Ordnance Survey® This product includes map data licensed from Ordnance Survey® with the permission of the Controller of Her Majesty's Stationery Office. © Crown copyright 2002. All rights reserved. Licence No: 399221.

Published by AA Publishing (a trading name of Automobile Association Developments Limited, whose registered office is Millstream, Maidenhead Road, Windsor, Berkshire SL4 5GD. Registered number 1878835).

The Post Office is a registered trademark of Post Office Ltd. in the UK and other countries.

Schools address data provided by Education Direct.

One-way street data provided by:

Tele Atlas ◄ © Tele Atlas N.V.

Mapping produced by the Cartographic Department of The Automobile Association. A01552

A CIP Catalogue record for this book is available from the British Library.

Printed by GRAFIASA S.A., Porto, Portugal

The contents of this atlas are believed to be correct at the time of the latest revision. However, the publishers cannot be held responsible for loss occasioned to any person acting or refraining from action as a result of any material in this atlas, nor for any errors, omissions or changes in such material. This does not affect your statutory rights. The publishers would welcome information to correct any errors or omissions and to keep this atlas up to date. Please write to Publishing, The Automobile Association, Fanum House (FH17), Basing View, Basingstoke, Hampshire, RG21 4EA.

Ref: ML219

Key to map pages	ii-iii
Key to map symbols	iv-1
Enlarged scale pages	2-3
Street by Street	4-41
Index – towns & villages	42
Index – streets	43-50
Index – featured places	51

ii

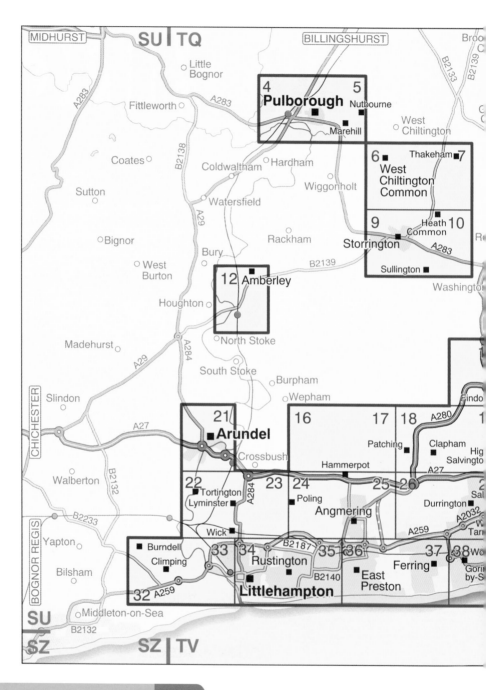

MIDHURST   SU TQ   BILLINGSHURST   Broo

Little Bognor

Fittleworth   A283   **4** Pulborough **5**   Nutbourne

West Chiltington

Coates   B2138   Coldwaltham   Hardham   Marehill

6 West Chiltington Common **7**   Thakeham

Sutton   Watersfield   Wiggonholt

A29   **9** Storrington Heath Common **10**   A283

Bignor   Bury   Rackham   Sullington   Washington

West Burton   **12** Amberley   B2139

Houghton   North Stoke

Madehurst   A284   South Stoke

Slindon   Burpham   Wepham   Findo

CHICHESTER   A27   **21** Arundel   **16** **17** **18** A280   1

Walberton   B2132   Crossbush   Hammerpot   Patching   Clapham   Hig Salvingto

22 Tortington Lyminster   A284   **23** **24** Poling Angmering   **25** **26**   Durrington   Sal

BOGNOR REGIS   B2233   Wick   A259   Tarr

Yapton   Burndell   **33** **34** Rustington   **35** **36** **37** **38** Wo   Gori by-S

Bilsham   Climping   B2187   East Preston   Ferring

32 A259   **Littlehampton**   B2140

Middleton-on-Sea   SU

SZ   B2132   SZ TV

Enlarged scale pages   1:10,000   6.3 inches to I mile

0   1/4   miles   1/2

0   1/4   1/2   kilometres   3/4   I

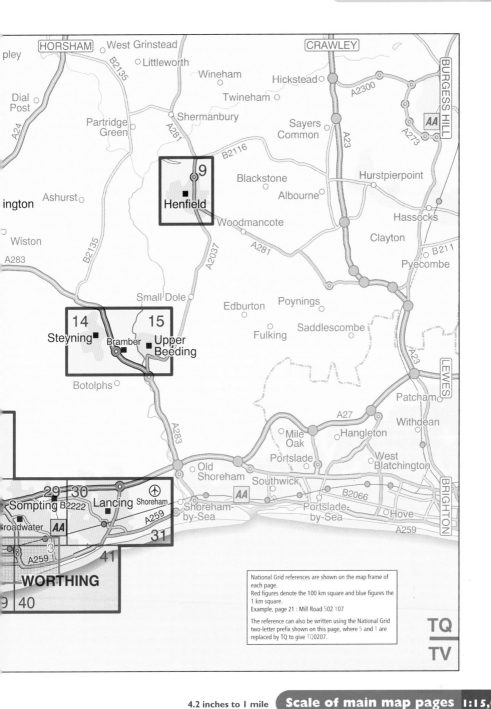

 pley

HORSHAM

West Grinstead

Littleworth

B2135

Dial
Post

Partridge
Green

A24

ington

Ashurst

Wiston

A283

B2135

Wineham

Shermanbury

A281

CRAWLEY

Hicksstead

A2300

Twineham

Sayers
Common

A23

A273

BURGESS HILL

AA

9

Henfield

Blackstone

Albourne

Hurstpierpoint

Hassocks

B2116

Woodmancote

A2037

A281

Clayton

B211

Pyecombe

Small Dole

Edburton

Poynings

14

Steyning

15

Upper
Beeding

Bramber

Botolphs

Fulking

Saddlescombe

A23

A283

LEWES

Patcham

A27

Withdean

Mile
Oak

Hangleton

West
Blatchington

Portslade

Old
Shoreham

Southwick

AA

B2066

BRIGHTON

29

30

Sompting

B2222

Lancing

Shoreham

Shoreham-
by-Sea

Portslade-
by-Sea

Hove

roadwater

AA

A259

31

A259

3

41

9

40

WORTHING

National Grid references are shown on the map frame of
each page.
Red figures denote the 100 km square and blue figures the
1 km square.
Example, page 21 : Mill Road 502 107

The reference can also be written using the National Grid
two-letter prefix shown on this page, where 5 and 1 are
replaced by TQ to give TQ0207.

TQ
—
TV

4.2 inches to 1 mile   Scale of main map pages 1:15,000

0   1/4   miles   1/2   3/4   1

0   1/4   1/2   kilometres 3/4   1   1 1/4   1 1/2

iv

Junction 9	Motorway & junction	⊖	Underground station
Services	Motorway service area	⊖	Light railway & station
	Primary road single/dual carriageway	+++++++++	Preserved private railway
Services	Primary road service area	LC	Level crossing
	A road single/dual carriageway	●—●—●—●	Tramway
	B road single/dual carriageway	- - - - - - - -	Ferry route
	Other road single/dual carriageway	··················	Airport runway
	Minor/private road, access may be restricted	— · — · — · —	County, administrative boundary
← ←	One-way street	▼▼▼▼▼▼▼▼▼	Mounds
	Pedestrian area	17	Page continuation 1:15,000
- - - - - - - -	Track or footpath	3	Page continuation to enlarged scale 1:10,000
	Road under construction		River/canal, lake, pier
⌐ - - = = ⌐	Road tunnel		Aqueduct, lock, weir
AA	AA Service Centre	465 ▲ Winter Hill	Peak (with height in metres)
P	Parking		Beach
P+🚌	Park & Ride		Woodland
🚌	Bus/coach station		Park
	Railway & main railway station		Cemetery
	Railway & minor railway station		Built-up area

	Featured building		Abbey, cathedral or priory
	City wall		Castle
A&E	Hospital with 24-hour A&E department		Historic house or building
PO	Post Office	Wakehurst Place NT	National Trust property
	Public library		Museum or art gallery
i	Tourist Information Centre		Roman antiquity
	Petrol station Major suppliers only		Ancient site, battlefield or monument
†	Church/chapel		Industrial interest
	Public toilets		Garden
	Toilet with disabled facilities		Arboretum
PH	Public house AA recommended		Farm or animal centre
	Restaurant AA inspected		Zoological or wildlife collection
	Theatre or performing arts centre		Bird collection
	Cinema		Nature reserve
	Golf course	V	Visitor or heritage centre
▲	Camping AA inspected		Country park
	Caravan Site AA inspected		Cave
	Camping & caravan site AA inspected		Windmill
	Theme park		Distillery, brewery or vineyard

4

A · Pythingdean · 504 · B · C · 05 · D

CH

Hill Farm Lane

Codmore Hill Farm

1

20

Coombelands Lane

2

Coombelands

Stane St Cl

STANE STREET

A29

Works

3

19

Coombelands

Lane

Aston Ri · Orchard Ww

New Place Rd

Cousins

LONDON ROAD

Sports & Rec Grnd

Larch

Amb Stat

Link

The

Wey South Path

Police Station

Church Pl

Rectory Ct

Pavilion

Rectory

4

Station Approach Industrial Estate

P

Lyntons

CHURCH HILL

Hotel

Rectory Lane

Chestnut Wk

PO

Surgery

Pulborough Station

P

STATION ROAD

LOWER

ST

A283

Wfr Edg

All Whf

Wfr

Arun Ct

Barn House La

B.C.

ROAD

Old Bridge

PULBOROUGH

P

PHAM

5

A29

LONDON ROAD

118

Wey South Path

A · 504 · B · LONDON ROAD · C · 05 · D

1 grid square represents 500 metres

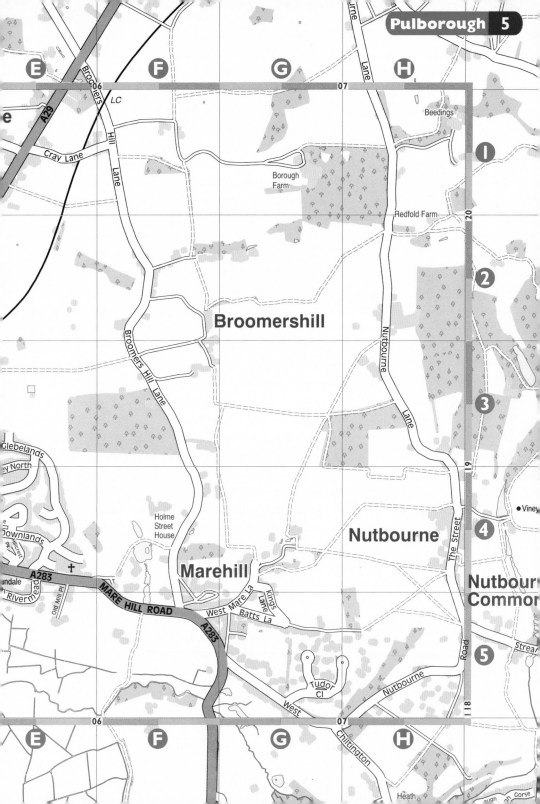

E F G H

LC

Beedings

A29

Cray Lane

Hill Lane

Brooters Hill

I

Borough Farm

Redfold Farm

20

2

Nutbourne Lane

Broomershill

3

Broomers Hill Lane

19

Glebelands

ey North

• Viney

Downlands

Holme Street House

Nutbourne

4

The Street

Pollcrest

†

A283

Nutbour Common

ndale

Rivermead

Old Mill Pl

Marehill

MARE HILL ROAD

West Mare La

Kings Lane

Road

Stream

A283

West Mare La

Batts La

5

118

Tudor Cl

Nutbourne

West

Chiltington

Heath

E F G H

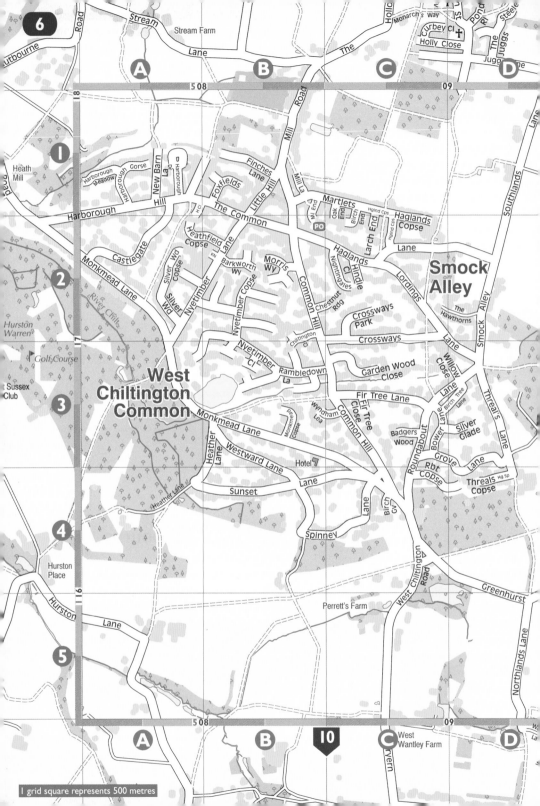

E F G H

I

Crays Farm

Cray's La

DUKE'S HILL

Town House Farm

ands

Thakeham First School

The Street

Thakeham

Cray's Lane

2

Thakeham Place

Hardbarrow Woods

High Bar Lane

Linfield Copse

Warminghurst

Furze Common Road

B2139

STORRINGTON ROAD

Abingworth

3

Champions Farm

4

Strawberry Lane

Park Barn

B2139

STORRINGTON ROAD

5

Merrywood Lane

Little Thakeham

Newhouse Farm

E F **11** G H

Crescent R

STORRINGTON ROAD

Newhouse

Melrose Place

Squirrel

Tudor Village

Mutton's

Lane

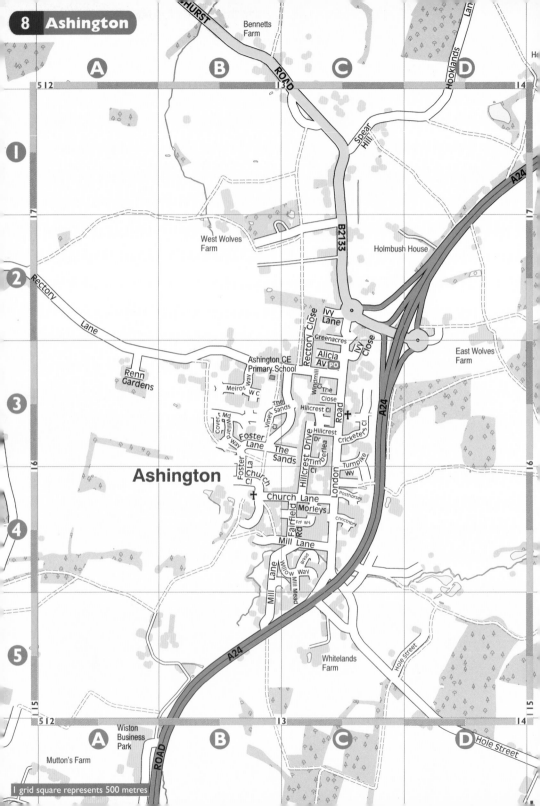

Bennetts Farm

A B C D

512 13 14

Lan

Hooklands

A24

Spear Hill

1

17

B2133

West Wolves Farm

Holmbush House

2

Rectory Lane

Ivy Lane

Rectory Close

Greenacres

Ivy Close

East Wolves Farm

Ashington CE Primary School

Alicia Av PO

Renn Gardens

Meiros

W C

The Close

Windmill

3

The Sands

Hillcrest Cl

Road

Viney

Covert

Md

Willard Way

Hillcrest

Dr

Cricketer's Cl

Ashington

Foster Lane

Bertlea

Tim Cl

Turnpike

16

The Sands

Hillcrest Drive

Wy

Foster La

Church Cl

London

Posthorses

Church Lane

Morleys

Fairfield Rd

Frf Wn

Chnctnbry

4

Mill Lane

Lane

Birch

Willow

Mill Mead

Way

Mill Lane

A24

5

Whitelands Farm

Hole Street

115 13 14 115

512

A B C D Hole Street

Wiston Business Park

ROAD

Mutton's Farm

1 grid square represents 500 metres

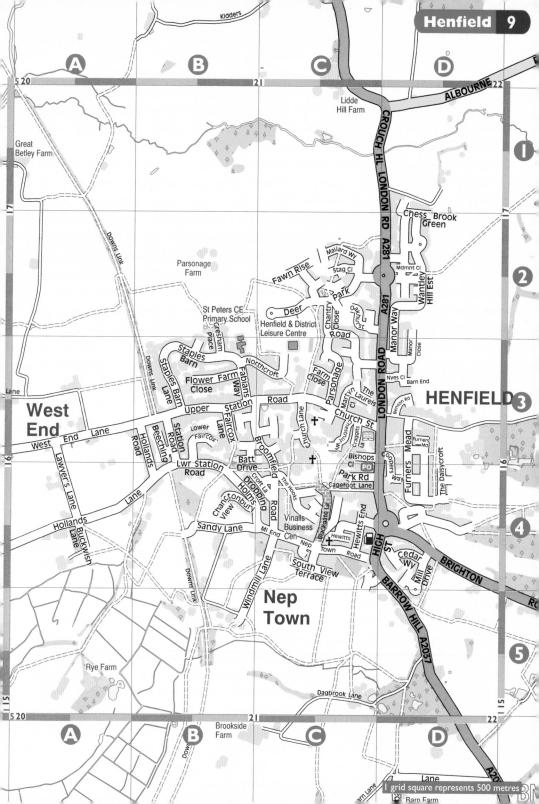

520 A 21 B C 22 D

ALBOURNE

Kidders

Lidde
Hill Farm

CROUCH HL

1

Great
Betley Farm

LONDON RD

Chess Brook
Green

17

Downs Link

Fawn Rise

Mallard Wy

A281

Mdmnt Cl

2

Parsonage
Farm

Stag Cl

Park

Manor Way

Wantley
Hill Est

St Peters CE
Primary School

Deer

Chantry
Close

Oak Cl

Manor
Close

Staples
Barn

Henfield & District
Leisure Centre

Road

Gresham
Place

Northcroft

Farm
Close

Nyes Cl

Barn End

HENFIELD 3

Staples Barn
Lane

Flower Farm
Close

Fabians
Way

Parsonage

Martyn Cl

The
Laurels

Benson Rd

16

West
End

Upper

Station
Lane

Faircox

Road

Church St

Cragits

Furners
Mead

The Daisycroft

West End Lane

Station
Road

Lower
Faircox

Broomfield

Church Lane

Furners
Md

Lawyer's Lane

Beeching
Road

Hollands

Lwr Station
Road

Batt
Drive

Croft La

The Hooks

Bishops
Cl

Park Rd

PO

Coopers
Way

Hollands

Buckwish
Lane

Lane

Dlopping
Road

Holmls

Chanctonbury
View

Sandy Lane

Ml End Lane

Vinalls
Business
Cen

Blackgate La

Cagefoot Lane

Hewitts End

Hewitts
Town Road

HIGH ST

Cedar
Wy

Mill
Drive

BRIGHTON

4

**Nep
Town**

Windmill Lane

south View
Terrace

Nep

BARROW HILL A2037

5

Rye Farm

Downs Link

Dagbrook Lane

Barn Farm

1115

520 A 21 B Brookside
Farm C 22 D

1 grid square represents 500 metres

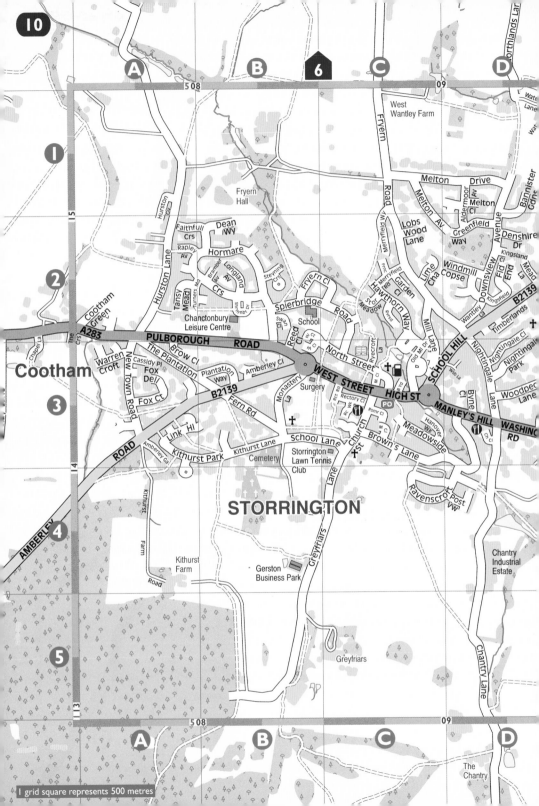

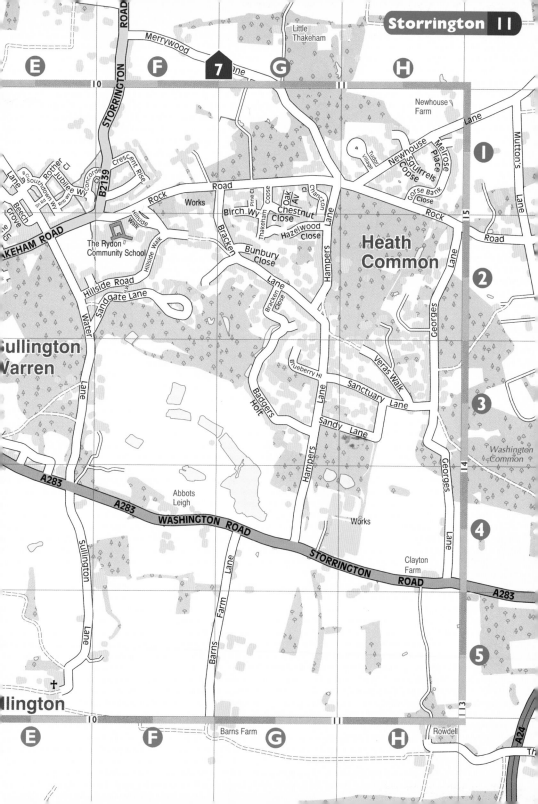

Little Thakeham

Merrywood

Newhouse Farm

E F **7** G H

Newhouse Squirrels Copse

Melrose Place

Gorse Bank Close

Tudor Village

Mutton's Lane

Lane

Rother Cl
Jubilee Wy
Concorde
Crescent Rise
B2139
Southdown Wy
Lane
Beech Grove
Cl

Rock Road

Works

Birch Wy
Pine Cl
Thakeham Copse
Oak Av
Chestnut Close
Hazelwood Close
Chanctor
Hampers Lane
Rock Road
Georges Lane

Hillside Walk
Hillside Walk
Bracken Lane
Bunbury Close

AKEHAM ROAD

The Rydon Community School

Hillside Road
Sandgate Lane
Water
Lane

Heath Common

Bracken Close
Lane

Bullington Warren

Badgers Holt
Lane
Blueberry Hl
Sanctuary Lane
Veras Walk

Georges Lane

Washington Common

Sandy Lane
Hampers Lane

A283
A283
WASHINGTON ROAD
STORRINGTON ROAD
A283

Sullington Lane

Abbots Leigh

Works

Clayton Farm

Georges Lane

Barns Farm Lane

†

lington

E 10 F G H

Barns Farm
Rowdell
A24
Th

I

2

3

4

5

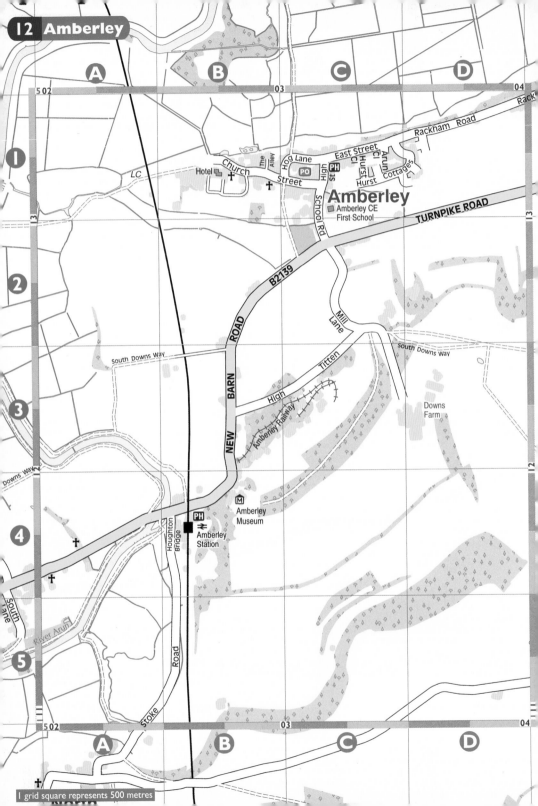

A B C D

5 02 03 04

Rack

Rackham Road

LC

Hotel
Church Street
The Alley
Hog Lane
East Street
Arun Cl
Hurst Cl
Hurst
Cottages
High St
PO
PH

Amberley

Amberley CE
First School

School Rd

TURNPIKE ROAD

B2139

Mill Lane

ROAD

South Downs Way

South Downs Way

BARN

Titten

Downs Farm

NEW

High

Amberley Railway

Downs Way

Amberley Museum

Houghton Bridge

PH

Amberley Station

South Lane

River Arun

Stoke Road

A B C D

5 02 03 04

1 grid square represents 500 metres

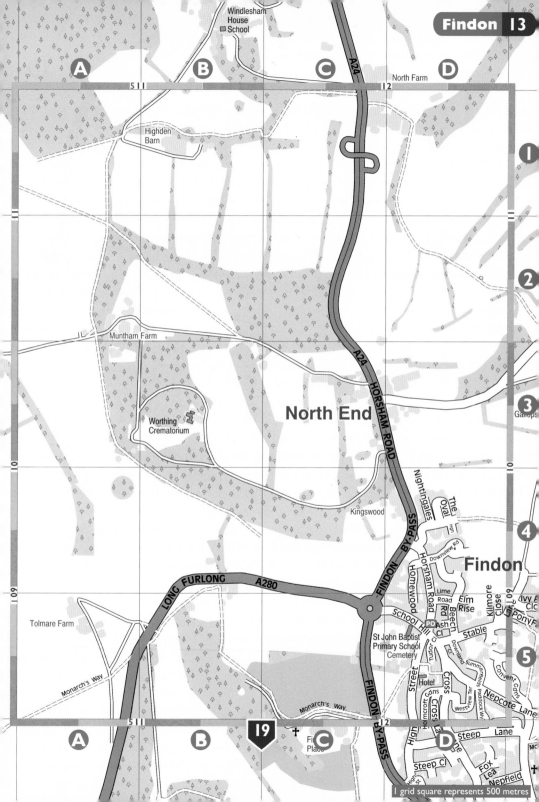

Windlesham
House
School

A B C D

A24

5 11 12 North Farm

Highden
Barn

I

Muntham Farm

2

North End

HORSHAM ROAD

A24

3

Gallops

Worthing
Crematorium

Kingswood

Nightingales

The
Oval

FINDON BY-PASS

4

Downview Rd

Horsham Road

Findon

LONG FURLONG A280

Homewood

Lime
Road

Elm
Rise

Ivy
Cl

Pony

0 10 0 6 0

Tolmare Farm

School Hill

PO

Ash
Cl

Beech
Rd

Stable

Kilmore
Close

Convent

St John Baptist
Primary School
Cemetery

5

Monarch's Way

Street

Hotel

Homecroft
Gdns

Cross
La

West View Ter

Downland

Paddock Wy

summerfields

Nepcote Lane

Monarch's Way

FINDON BY-PASS

5 11 12

A B 19 C Fi
Place D Steep Lane

Fox
Lea

Nepfield

Steep Cl

1 grid square represents 500 metres

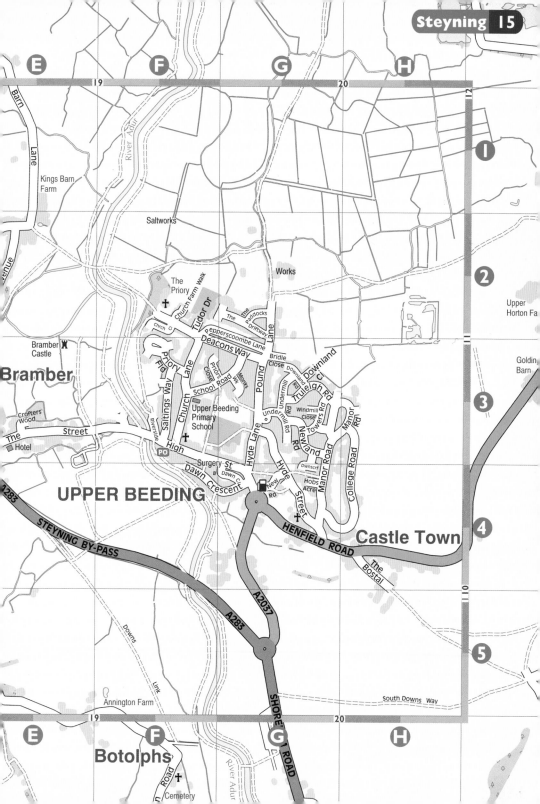

E F G H

19 20

I

2

1

Barn Lane

River Adur

Kings Barn Farm

Saltworks

Works

Upper Horton Fa

Goldin Barn

The Priory

Church Farm Walk

Tudor Dr

Pepperscoombe Lane

The Paddocks

The Driftway

Chrch Cl

Bramber Castle

Bramber

Priory Fld

Priory Lane

Church Lane

Deacons Way

Priors Close

Works

School Road

Bridle Close

Downland

Downland

Truleigh Rd

Pound Lane

Lane

C
L

Saltings Way

Riverside

Upper Beeding Primary School

Undermill Rd

Undermill Rd

Windmill Close

Towers Rd

Manor Rd

Goldin Barn

Crofters Wood

The Street

High

PO

Hyde Lane

Newland Rd

Downscrft

Manor Road

College Road

The Hotel

Surgery St

Dawn Cl

Dawn Crescent

New Rd

Hyde Street

Hobs Acre

3

UPPER BEEDING

A1283

STEYNING BY-PASS

A283

A2037

Link

Annington Farm

Downs

Castle Town

HENFIELD ROAD

The Bostal

110

4

5

South Downs Way

E F G H

19 20

Botolphs

Road

SHORE ROAD

River Adur

Cemetery

Ⓐ Ⓑ Ⓒ Ⓓ

Wepham   5 05   06

1

80

New Down

2

Wepham Wood

3

07

4

Blakehurst Lane

5

The Dover

Priorsleas Farm

06

5 05

109

Ⓐ Ⓑ **24** Ⓒ Ⓓ

A27   **ARUN**

Newplace

Beling

E F G H

07 08

Monarch's Way

Michelgrove

I

2

3

18

4

5

Monarch's Way

Monarch's Way

Angmering Park

Angmering Park Farm

Norfolk House

Selden Farm

Swillage Lane

Selden Lane

France Lane

Selden

E F G H

07 25 08

Hammerpot
PH

Arundel Road

A B C D

Monarch's Way 5 09 10

Myrtle Grove
Farm

1

Monarch's Way

BN13

Longfurlong Lane

2

LONG FURLONG A280 Longfurlong
Barn

A280

3

17

07

Street

4

The

† Patching

†

Church Cl.

Coldharbour Lane Street Weir Cl.

The

PO

5

Clapham & Patching CE
Primary School

LONG FURLONG

Clapham

106

France Lane

Selden 5 09 10

A B C D

A280

26 Holt F

Clapham Common

A27

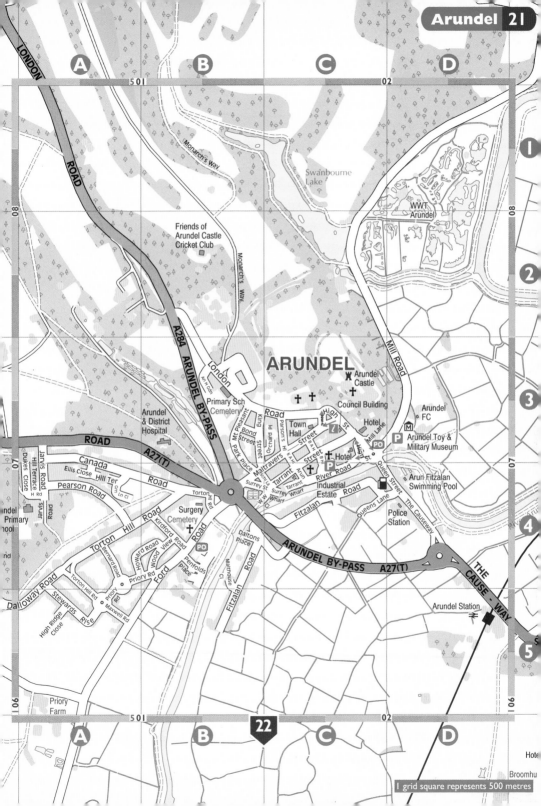

LONDON ROAD

Monarch's Way

Swanbourne Lake

WWT Arundel

A284 ARUNDEL BY-PASS

Friends of Arundel Castle Cricket Club

Monarch's Way

ARUNDEL

Arundel Castle

London

Art H Gdn

Primary Sch Cemetery

Council Building

Arundel FC

Arundel & District Hospital

Mt Pleasant

Bond Street

Park Place

King Street

Orchard St

Parsons' H

High St

Town Hall

Road

Hotel

Mill Lane

PO

Arundel Toy & Military Museum

ROAD

A27(T)

Canada

Hill Ter

Road

Ellis Close

Jarvis Road

Dukes Close

Hill Terrace

Jarvis Rd

Pearson Road

Jarvis Road

Maltravers

Surrey St

Tarrant

Surrey Wharf

Surrey Wharf

Tarrant Wharf

River Road

Arun Fitzalan Swimming Pool

Industrial Estate

Road

Queen Street

The Causeway

Police Station

Torton

Hill Rd

Surgery

Cemetery

Fitzalan

Queens Lane

Hill Rd

Torton Hill Road

Kirdford Road

Howard Road

Bernard Road

Wood View Road

PO

Daltons Place

Penfolds Place

Maltravers

ARUNDEL BY-PASS A27(T)

THE CAUSE-WAY

Dalloway Road

Stewards Rise

High Ridge Close

Torton Hill Rd

Priory Rd

Priory Rd

Maxwell Rd

Ford

Fitzalan Road

Arundel Station

Priory Farm

Broomhu

Hote

1 grid square represents 500 metres

A Priory Farm

501

B

21

C

02

D

I

05

Tortington

2

Ford Road

†

River Arun

3

Church Lane

Church

†

Works

er Way

LC

4

Kingsmead

Arundel Drive

Old Mead

104

ip &
nchor

Brook
Barn Farm

Courtwick

Wick

5

†

Swift Wy

Robin Cl

Finches

Kingfisher Dr

Coldcrest Av

Courtwick

La

Court
Wick
Park

NW Crook La

Waters
Business
Park

501

A

B

02

33

C

D

Willow
Brook

Joyce Cl

Wheatcroft

Stea
Furlo

Courtwick

Greenfields

Clun Road

The
Crossway

River Arun

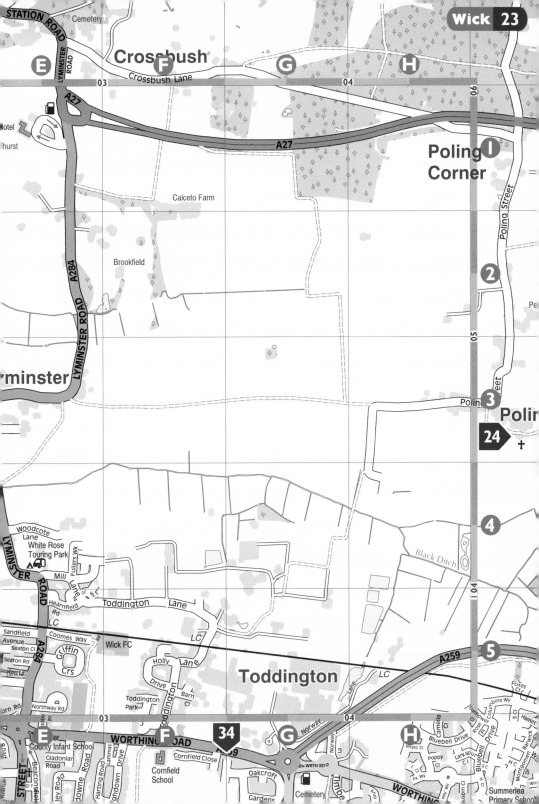

A 5 05 B 16 C Priorsleas Farm D

A27 ARUND

Poling
Corner

Poling Street

Newplace
Farm

2

Peckhams

3 Poling

Poling

ANGMERIN

Old Place
Farm

That

4

BN16

Black Ditch

The

Golf Course

Ham Manor
Golf Club

Golf Course

Manor

5

Ham
Manor Farm

Blue Cedars Cl

Ham Manor Cl

West Drive

East

06

Foxes
Cl

Brook La

Brook Lane

South Drive

Camelia
Cl

Bluebell Drive

Rose

Hamilton Dr

Drewetts Cl

Blenheim Dr

Poppy
Cl

Bluebell Drive

Windsor

Cowdray Drive

Pentola

Dominion Way

A Rustington
Trading
Estate

B 35 C D

NEW ROAD

Rustington

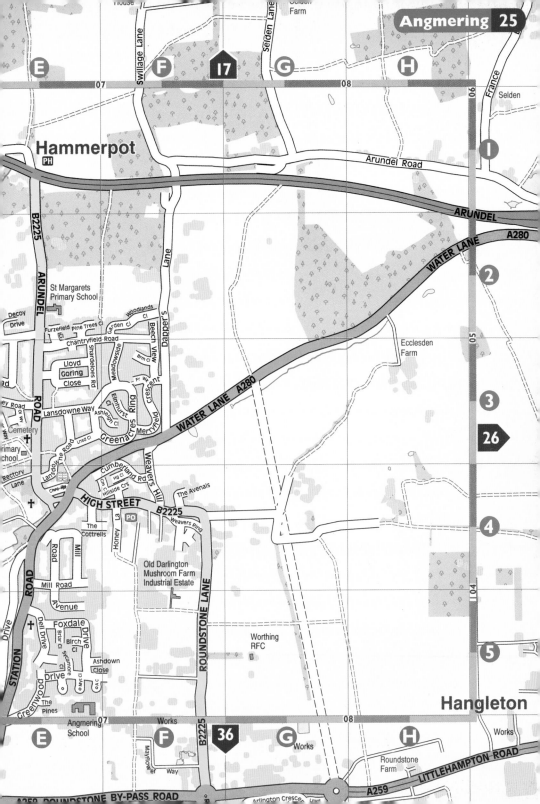

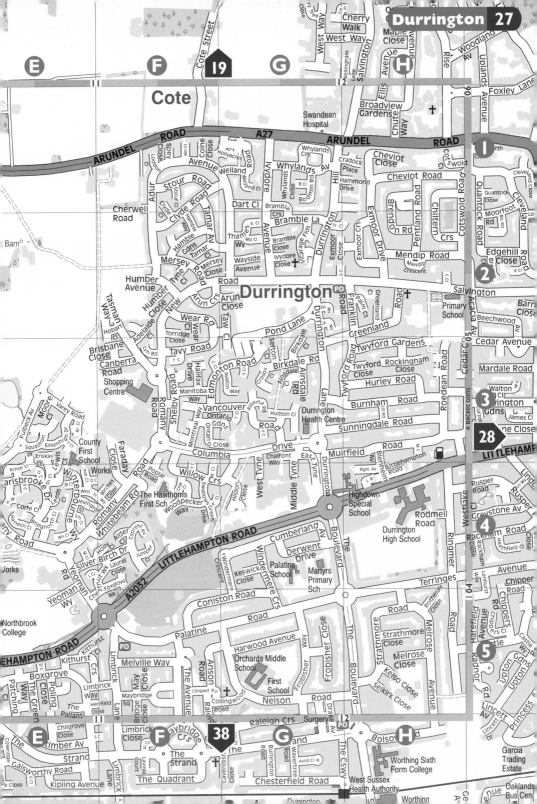

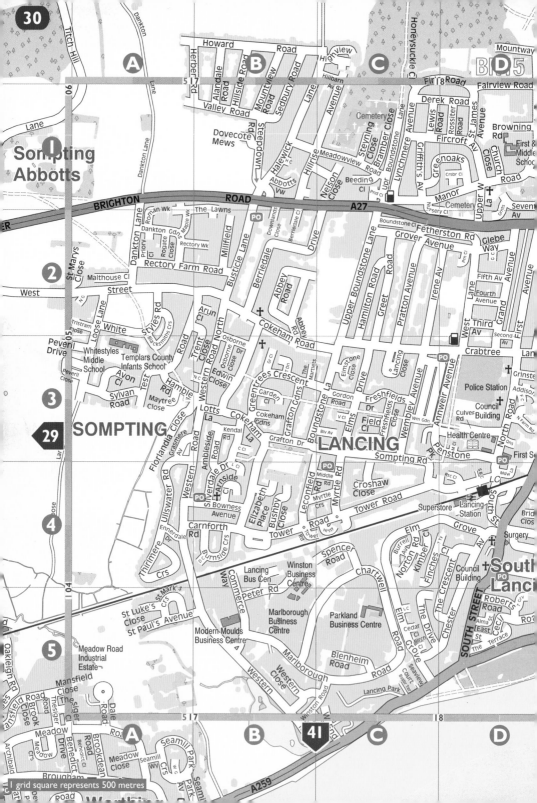

The Drive
Coombes Rd
Coombes Rd
A27
Works

Hoe

E
F
G
H

Boxgrove
Close
Swanbourne
Close
Norbury
Close
The
Moorings

19
20
90

OLD SHOREHAM ROAD
Old Shoreham Road
A27
Almond
Avenue

Court

th
ncing

I

Old Shoreham Rd

Lewin
Close

Manor
Close

Cecil Pashley Way

Manor
Way
Hayley
Road
Road
Lisher Road
Irvins
Woodard
Rd
MC
Shadwells
Close
Daniel
Close
Gravelly Crs
Shadwells Crs

Shoreham
Airport

D-Day
Museum
M

2

05

Cecil Pashley Way

Barfield Park
Hadlow
Way
Links
Road
's Avenue
North Farm
Road
Close

New Salts Farm Road

3

Old Salts Farm Road

Windsor Regent Millennium Cl
Downs Cl
Drakes Cl
Haigh Cl
Manor Cl
Abbey Cl
The Broadway
Sussex Rd
Orient Rd
Swallows Cl
Adur Cl

Kings Crs
Kings
Gap
Works
P

The Paddocks
Freshbrook
Brook Way
Road
Larkfield Close
Road
Salts Farm Road
Boundary Road
West Avenue
Prince Way
George V Avenue
Bristol Avenue

PO
A259

West Beach Road
4

The Close
Seaside Road
Seaside Cl
Thornberry Middle School
West Avenue
West Avenue

104

Seaside
Avenue
Alexandra
Rd
Queens Rd
Crs
leigh Cl
The Close
The Fairway
T Sit

The Fairway
Old Salts Road

BRIGHTON
ROAD
Shopsdam Road

5

E
F
G
H
19
20

A   **B**   **C**   **D**

499   500

Park

Ford Lane   Ford La   Ford Rd

✝

Ford

Rodney Crs   Rodney Crs

I

Ford Airfield
Industrial
Estate

Downview Road

Goodnew Close

Burndell

Lewis Lane

Ford

Nelson Row

03

Fordwater
Gardens

Mustang Cl

Beagle Dr

Park

Johnson Way

Drake Groove

Wills Close

Sproule Cl

Douglas Close

Rollaston

Road

BURNDELL ROAD

Climping

irholme

2

Miles Cl

Junction
Close

B2233

Rudford
Industrial
Estate

Rudford
Industrial
Estate

✝

YAPTON

Church

**Horsemere
Green**

Gn Lane

3

02

Horsemere

Wk

Mant
Cl

Wooldridge

Apple
Tree
Walk

ROAD

A259

CROOKTHORN   **CROOKTHORN LANE**

St Marys
Primary S

4

CROOKTHORN
LA

Climping
Street

GREVATT'S   LANE

Climping

5

01

Ryebank Rife

Street

D

Hotel

499   500

A   **B**   **C**   **D**

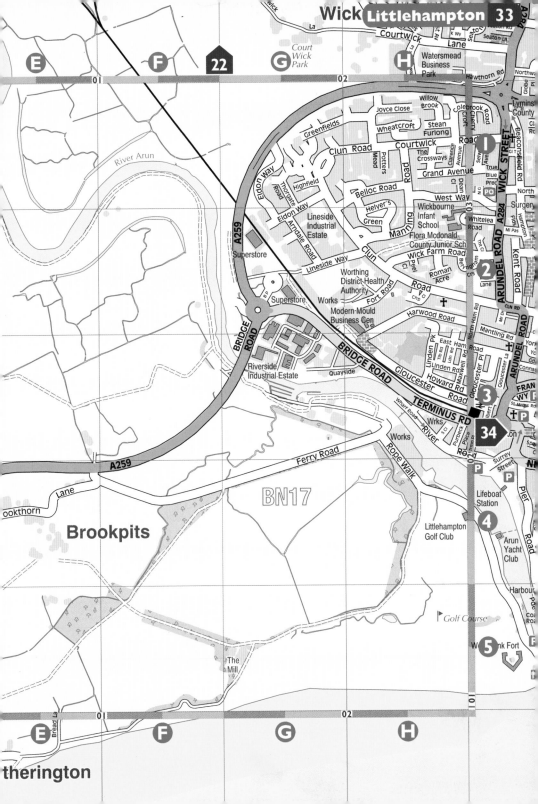

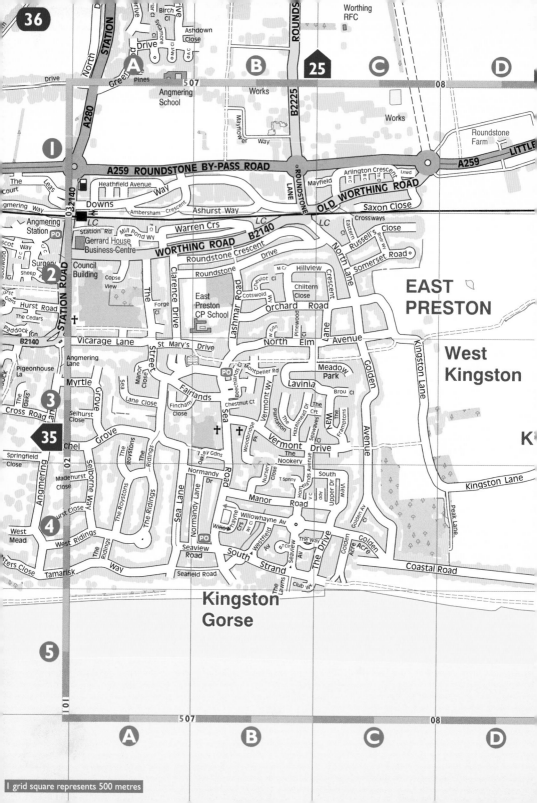

1 grid square represents 500 metres

Abingworth	7 F3	East Kingston	36 D3
Amberley	12 C1	East Preston	36 C2
Angmering	24 D3	East Worthing	41 E1
Arundel	21 G3	Ferring	37 G2
Ashington	8 A4	Findon	13 H4
Bramber	15 E3	Findon Valley	20 C4
Broadwater	29 E3	Goring-by-Sea	38 C1
Brookpits	33 E4	Hammerpot	25 E1
Broomershill	5 F2	Hangleton	25 H5
Burndell	32 A1	Heath Common	11 H2
Castle Town	15 H4	Henfield	9 H3
Clapham	18 C5	High Salvington	19 F5
Climping	32 C2	Horsemere Green	32 B3
Codmore Hill	4 D1	Kingston Gorse	36 B5
Cote	27 F1	Lancing	30 C3
Durrington	27 G2	Littlehampton	34 B3

Lyminster	23 E3	South Lancing	
Marehill	5 F4	Steyning	
Nepcote	20 A1	Storrington	
Nep Town	9 G5	Sullington	
North End	13 G3	Sullington Warren	
North Lancing	31 E1	Thakeham	
Nutbourne	5 H4	Toddington	
Patching	18 A4	Upper Beeding	
Poling	24 A3	Warminghurst	
Poling Corner	23 H1	West Chiltington Common	
Pulborough	4 C5	West End	
Rustington	35 G3	West Kingston	
Salvington	28 B2	West Tarring	
Smock Alley	6 C2	West Worthing	
Sompting	30 A3	Wick	
Sompting Abbotts	29 H1	Worthing	

USING THE STREET INDEX

Street names are listed alphabetically. Each street name is followed by its postal town or area locality, the Postcode District, the page number, and the reference to the square in which the name is found.

Standard index entries are shown as follows:

Abbey Cl *LAN/SOMP* BN15 ....**31** G3

Street names and selected addresses not shown on the map due to scale restrictions are shown in the index with an asterisk:

Abingdon Ldg *ANG/EP* * BN16........**35** G3

GENERAL ABBREVIATIONS

ACC	ACCESS	E	EAST	LDG	LODGE	R	F
ALY	ALLEY	EMB	EMBANKMENT	LGT	LIGHT	RBT	ROUNDAI
AP	APPROACH	EMBY	EMBASSY	LK	LOCK	RD	F
AR	ARCADE	ESP	ESPLANADE	LKS	LAKES	RDG	R
ASS	ASSOCIATION	EST	ESTATE	LNDG	LANDING	REP	REPL
AV	AVENUE	EX	EXCHANGE	LTL	LITTLE	RES	RESER
BCH	BEACH	EXPY	EXPRESSWAY	LWR	LOWER	RFC	RUGBY FOOTBALL
BLDS	BUILDINGS	EXT	EXTENSION	MAG	MAGISTRATE	RI	
BND	BEND	F/O	FLYOVER	MAN	MANSIONS	RP	F
BNK	BANK	FC	FOOTBALL CLUB	MD	MEAD	RW	
BR	BRIDGE	FK	FORK	MDW	MEADOWS	S	SC
BRK	BROOK	FLD	FIELD	MEM	MEMORIAL	SCH	SCH
BTM	BOTTOM	FLDS	FIELDS	MKT	MARKET	SE	SOUTH
BUS	BUSINESS	FLS	FALLS	MKTS	MARKETS	SER	SERVICE
BVD	BOULEVARD	FLS	FLATS	ML	MALL	SH	SH
BY	BYPASS	FM	FARM	ML	MILL	SHOP	SHOP
CATH	CATHEDRAL	FT	FORT	MNR	MANOR	SKWY	SKY
CEM	CEMETERY	FWY	FREEWAY	MS	MEWS	SMT	SUI
CEN	CENTRE	FY	FERRY	MSN	MISSION	SOC	SOC
CFT	CROFT	GA	GATE	MT	MOUNT	SP	
CH	CHURCH	GAL	GALLERY	MTN	MOUNTAIN	SPR	SP
CHA	CHASE	GDN	GARDEN	MTS	MOUNTAINS	SQ	SO
CHYD	CHURCHYARD	GDNS	GARDENS	MUS	MUSEUM	ST	ST
CIR	CIRCLE	GLD	GLADE	MWY	MOTORWAY	STN	STA
CIRC	CIRCUS	GLN	GLEN	N	NORTH	STR	STR
CL	CLOSE	GN	GREEN	NE	NORTH EAST	STRD	STR
CLFS	CLIFFS	GND	GROUND	NW	NORTH WEST	SW	SOUTH
CMP	CAMP	GRA	GRANGE	O/P	OVERPASS	TDG	TRA
CNR	CORNER	GRG	GARAGE	OFF	OFFICE	TER	TER
CO	COUNTY	GT	GREAT	ORCH	ORCHARD	THWY	THROUGH
COLL	COLLEGE	GTWY	GATEWAY	OV	OVAL	TNL	TUI
COM	COMMON	GV	GROVE	PAL	PALACE	TOLL	TOL
COMM	COMMISSION	HGR	HIGHER	PAS	PASSAGE	TPK	TURN
CON	CONVENT	HL	HILL	PAV	PAVILION	TR	TI
COT	COTTAGE	HLS	HILLS	PDE	PARADE	TRL	TRL
COTS	COTTAGES	HO	HOUSE	PH	PUBLIC HOUSE	TWR	TC
CP	CAPE	HOL	HOLLOW	PK	PARK	U/P	UNDER
CPS	COPSE	HOSP	HOSPITAL	PKWY	PARKWAY	UNI	UNIVEF
CR	CREEK	HRB	HARBOUR	PL	PLACE	UPR	UI
CREM	CREMATORIUM	HTH	HEATH	PLN	PLAIN	V	
CRS	CRESCENT	HTS	HEIGHTS	PLNS	PLAINS	VA	VA
CSWY	CAUSEWAY	HVN	HAVEN	PLZ	PLAZA	VIAD	VIA
CT	COURT	HWY	HIGHWAY	POL	POLICE STATION	VIL	
CTRL	CENTRAL	IMP	IMPERIAL	PR	PRINCE	VIS	
CTS	COURTS	IN	INLET	PREC	PRECINCT	VLG	VILI
CTYD	COURTYARD	IND EST	INDUSTRIAL ESTATE	PREP	PREPARATORY	VLS	V
CUTT	CUTTINGS	INF	INFIRMARY	PRIM	PRIMARY	VW	
CV	COVE	INFO	INFORMATION	PROM	PROMENADE	W	
CYN	CANYON	INT	INTERCHANGE	PRS	PRINCESS	WD	W
DEPT	DEPARTMENT	IS	ISLAND	PRT	PORT	WHF	W
DL	DALE	JCT	JUNCTION	PT	POINT	WK	W
DM	DAM	JTY	JETTY	PTH	PATH	WKS	W
DR	DRIVE	KG	KING	PZ	PIAZZA	WLS	W
DRO	DROVE	KNL	KNOLL	QD	QUADRANT	WY	
DRY	DRIVEWAY	L	LAKE	QU	QUEEN	YD	Y
DWGS	DWELLINGS	LA	LANE	QY	QUAY	YHA	YOUTH HC

POSTCODE TOWNS AND AREA ABBREVIATIONS

ANG/EP	Angmering/East Preston	HFD	Henfield	PUL/STOR	Pulborough/Storrington	WTHG	Wo
ARUN	Arundel	LAN/SOMP	Lancing/Sompting	SALV	Salvington		
FERR	Ferring	LHPTN	Littlehampton	SHOR	Shoreham		
FIN/BW	Findon/Broadwater	MSEA/BNM	Middleton-on-Sea/Barnham	STEY/UB	Steyning/Upper Beeding		

A

ey Cl LAN/SOMP BN15 .....31 G3
ey Rd LAN/SOMP BN15 .....30 B3
TEY/UB BN44 .....14 C1
THG BN11 .....2 B7
otswood Wk ANG/EP BN16 .....35 F4
otts Cl WTHG BN11 .....2 D4
otts Vw LAN/SOMP BN15 .....30 B1
otts Wy LAN/SOMP BN15 .....31 E3
cket Gdns SALV BN13 .....28 A3
gdon Ldg ANG/EP * BN16 .....35 G3
cia Av SALV BN13 .....28 A2
rn Cl ANG/EP BN16 .....25 E5
Acre WTHG BN11 .....2 A5
rn Cl ANG/EP BN16 .....35 E2
aide Cl SALV BN13 .....27 F3
irals Wk ANG/EP BN16 .....34 D2
r Av SALV BN13 .....27 F1
r Cl LAN/SOMP BN15 .....31 H4
r Valley Ct STEY/UB * BN44 .....15 C3
r Vw STEY/UB * BN44 .....15 F3
ersane Rd FIN/BW BN14 .....28 C4
aia Rd WTHG BN11 .....39 E3
sdale Cl SALV BN13 .....27 E2
sdale Rd SALV BN13 .....27 G3
sdale Rd LAN/SOMP BN15 .....30 B1
rn Cl ANG/EP BN16 .....39 F3
erta Rd SALV BN13 .....27 G3
ert Rd ANG/EP BN16 .....35 F2
PTN BN17 .....34 A3
ourne Rd HFD BN5 .....9 H1
er Cl SALV BN13 .....27 F4
ermoor Av PUL/STOR RH20 .....10 D2
erney Rd FERR BN12 .....37 G4
sworth Av FERR BN12 .....38 A2
sworth Ct FERR BN12 .....38 A2
sworth Pde FERR * BN12 .....38 A2
wick Cl ANG/EP BN16 .....35 E5
wick Crs FIN/BW BN14 .....20 B5
xander Ter WTHG * BN11 .....3 F5
xandra Ct FERR BN12 .....38 B1
xandra Rd LAN/SOMP BN15 .....31 K4
THG BN11 .....3 K4
ard Cl FIN/BW BN14 .....28 B2
Alley ARUN BN18 .....12 B1
eys Whf PUL/STOR RH20 .....4 C4
gdon Rd FIN/BW BN14 .....29 F2
a St LAN/SOMP BN15 .....30 D5
ond Av SHOR BN43 .....31 H1
na Cottages
UL/STOR * RH20 .....5 E4
erstone Rd WTHG BN11 .....3 J2
erley Cl LHPTN BN17 .....34 B2
UL/STOR RH20 .....10 B3
erley Ga PUL/STOR RH20 .....10 A3
erley Rd FIN/BW BN14 .....35 F4
ersham Crs ANG/EP BN16 .....36 A3
oleside Rd LAN/SOMP BN15 .....30 B4
brose Pl WTHG BN11 .....2 E4
elia Rd WTHG BN11 .....2 D4
hor Ct FERR BN12 .....38 D3
hor Springs LHPTN BN17 .....34 A3
ren Cl FERR BN12 .....26 C5
sisters Rd FERR BN12 .....37 F3
son Ct FERR * BN12 .....27 F5
son Rd FERR BN12 .....27 F5
pletrees ANG/EP BN16 .....36 C4
le Tree Wk LHPTN BN17 .....32 C5
il Cl FERR BN12 .....37 F4
Wy SALV BN13 .....26 D4

Arcade Buildings WTHG * BN11 .....3 F6
Arcade Rd LHPTN BN17 .....34 A3
Archibald Rd WTHG BN11 .....40 D1
Ardale Cl WTHG BN11 .....39 E2
Ardingly Dr FERR BN12 .....38 A1
Ardsheal Cl FIN/BW BN14 .....28 D4
Ardsheal Rd FIN/BW BN14 .....28 D4
Ariadne Rd WTHG BN11 .....2 A7
Arlington Av FERR BN12 .....38 A4
Arlington Cl FERR BN12 .....38 A4
Arlington Crs ANG/EP BN16 .....36 C1
Armada Wy ANG/EP BN16 .....35 E1
Arndale Rd LHPTN BN17 .....33 G2
Arnside Cl LAN/SOMP BN15 .....30 B4
Artex Av ANG/EP BN16 .....35 F1
Arun Cl ANG/EP * BN16 .....35 F2
   ARUN BN18 .....12 C1
   LAN/SOMP BN15 .....30 B2
   SALV BN13 .....27 G2
Arun Ct ANG/EP * BN16 .....35 F2
   PUL/STOR RH20 .....4 D4
Arun Crs SALV BN13 .....27 G2
Arundel By-Pass ARUN BN18 .....21 F3
Arundel Dr FERR BN12 .....38 A1
Arundel Rd FERR BN12 .....24 D1
   LHPTN BN17 .....34 A3
   SALV BN13 .....27 E1
Arun Pde LHPTN BN17 .....34 A5
Arun Prospect PUL/STOR * RH20 .....4 A5
Arun St ARUN BN18 .....21 G4
Arun Ter ARUN * BN18 .....21 G4
Ascot Wy ANG/EP BN16 .....35 H2
Ashacre La SALV BN13 .....28 A2
Ashacre Ms SALV BN13 .....28 A2
Ashburnham Cl SALV BN13 .....27 E4
Ash Cl FIN/BW BN14 .....13 H5
Ashdown Cl ANG/EP BN16 .....25 E3
Ashdown Rd WTHG BN11 .....3 F2
Ashfold Av FIN/BW BN14 .....20 B5
Ashv Cv WTHG BN11 .....2 A3
Ash La ANG/EP BN16 .....35 F3
Ashleigh Cl ANG/EP BN16 .....25 E3
Ashton Gdns ANG/EP BN16 .....35 F4
Ashurst Cl FERR BN12 .....38 A3
Ashurst Dr FERR BN12 .....38 A3
Ashurst Wy ANG/EP BN16 .....36 A2
Ashwood Cl WTHG BN11 .....3 K1
Ashwood Dr ANG/EP BN16 .....35 F3
Aspen Ct LAN/SOMP * BN15 .....30 D5
Aston Ri PUL/STOR RH20 .....4 D3
Athelstan Rd SALV BN13 .....28 A3
Augusta Pl WTHG BN11 .....2 E6
Avalon Wy SALV BN13 .....28 A3
The Avenals ANG/EP BN16 .....25 F4
The Avenue FERR BN12 .....38 B4
Avon Cl LAN/SOMP BN15 .....30 A3
Avondale Cl FERR BN12 .....38 C1
Avon Rd LHPTN BN17 .....34 A3

B

Badgers Holt PUL/STOR RH20 .....11 G3
Badgers Wd PUL/STOR RH20 .....6 C3
Bailey Cl ANG/EP BN16 .....25 E1
Bakers Arms Hl ARUN BN18 .....21 F3
Balcombe Av FIN/BW BN14 .....28 D4
Banjo Rd LHPTN BN17 .....34 B5
Bank Pas STEY/UB BN44 .....14 C1
Banks Cft PUL/STOR RH20 .....10 D2
Bannister Gdns PUL/STOR RH20 .....11 H3
Banstead Ct FERR BN12 .....38 B3
Barbary La FERR BN12 .....37 F3
Barfield Pk LAN/SOMP BN15 .....31 H5
Barkworth Wy PUL/STOR RH20 .....6 B2
Barn Cl FERR BN12 .....37 G3
   SALV BN13 .....28 A2
Barn End HFD BN5 .....9 H3
Barnhouse La PUL/STOR RH20 .....4 D1
Barn House La PUL/STOR RH20 .....4 D5
Barns Farm La PUL/STOR RH20 .....11 G3
Barnsite Gdns ANG/EP BN16 .....35 E2
Barque Cl ANG/EP BN16 .....35 E2
Barrington Cl FERR BN12 .....38 C2
Barrington La FERR BN12 .....38 B2
Barrow Hl HFD BN5 .....9 H5
Barton Cl SALV BN13 .....28 A2
Barwick Cl ANG/EP BN16 .....35 E1
Bashfords La FIN/BW BN14 .....29 E3
Batemans Cl SALV BN13 .....27 E4
Bath Pl WTHG BN11 .....3 H2
Bath Rd WTHG BN11 .....2 A7
Batts Dr HFD BN5 .....9 H3
Batts La PUL/STOR RH20 .....5 G5
Bayford Rd LHPTN BN17 .....34 A4
Bay Tree Gdn ANG/EP BN16 .....36 A3

Beach Crs LHPTN BN17 .....34 B5
Beachcroft Pl LAN/SOMP BN15 .....30 D5
Beach Pde WTHG BN11 .....3 H5
Beach Rd LHPTN BN17 .....34 B4
The Beaches LHPTN * BN17 .....32 C3
Beachside Cl FERR BN12 .....38 D3
Beaconsfield Rd LHPTN BN17 .....34 A1
Beagle Dr ARUN BN18 .....32 A2
Beaumont Pk LHPTN BN17 .....34 B4
Beaumont Rd FIN/BW BN14 .....29 E4
Beccles Rd WTHG BN11 .....2 B1
Becket Rd FIN/BW BN14 .....39 F1
Beckworth Cl SALV BN13 .....27 E4
Bedford Rw WTHG BN11 .....3 G5
Beech Cl FIN/BW * BN14 .....13 H4
Beeches Av FIN/BW BN14 .....29 E3
Beech Gv ANG/EP * BN15 .....31 E4
   PUL/STOR RH20 .....11 E1
Beechings HFD BN5 .....9 F3
Beechlands Cl ANG/EP BN16 .....36 B3
Beech Rd FIN/BW BN14 .....13 H5
Beech Vw ANG/EP BN16 .....25 F3
Beechwood Av SALV BN13 .....28 A2
Beeding Cl LAN/SOMP BN15 .....30 C1
Beehive Cl FERR BN12 .....37 G3
Beehive La FERR BN12 .....37 F3
Bell Davies Rd LHPTN BN17 .....34 C2
Belle Vue WTHG * BN11 .....2 E4
Belloc Rd LHPTN BN17 .....33 H1
Bellscroft Pl LHPTN BN17 .....34 C2
Bellview Rd SALV BN13 .....28 B4
Belsize Cl WTHG BN11 .....2 A3
Belsize Rd WTHG BN11 .....2 A3
Belvedere Av LAN/SOMP BN15 .....30 C3
Belyngham Crs LHPTN BN17 .....33 H2
Benedict Cl WTHG BN11 .....41 E1
Benedict Dr WTHG BN11 .....40 D1
Benson Rd HFD BN5 .....9 H3
Berkeley Sq WTHG BN11 .....39 F2
Berkshire Ct FERR * BN12 .....38 A1
Bernard Rd ARUN BN18 .....21 E4
   WTHG BN11 .....39 E3
Berriedale Cl LAN/SOMP BN15 .....30 B2
Berriedale Dr LAN/SOMP BN15 .....30 B2
Berry La LHPTN BN17 .....34 C4
Bessborough Ter
   LAN/SOMP BN15 .....30 C5
Beverley Gdns ANG/EP BN16 .....35 G5
Bewley Rd ANG/EP BN16 .....25 E3
Bignor Cl ANG/EP BN16 .....35 G2
Binsted Cl ANG/EP BN16 .....25 E5
Birch Cl ANG/EP BN16 .....25 E5
   LAN/SOMP BN15 .....30 C5
Birch End PUL/STOR RH20 .....6 C3
Birches Cl SALV BN13 .....27 F4
Birch Gv PUL/STOR RH20 .....6 C3
Birch Tree La PUL/STOR RH20 .....6 C3
Birch Wy PUL/STOR RH20 .....11 G2
Birkdale Cl SALV BN13 .....27 G3
Birkdale Rd SALV BN13 .....27 G3
Biscay Cl ANG/EP BN16 .....35 E2
Bishops Cl HFD BN5 .....9 G3
   SALV BN13 .....28 B3
Blackdown Rd SALV BN13 .....28 A2
Blackgate La HFD BN5 .....9 H5
Blacksmiths Cl PUL/STOR * RH20 .....8 C4
Blacksmiths Crs
   LAN/SOMP BN15 .....30 A3
Blakehurst La ARUN BN18 .....16 A3
Blakehurst Wy LHPTN BN17 .....34 A2
The Blatchen LHPTN BN17 .....34 C4
Blenheim Cl SALV BN13 .....27 H3
Blenheim Cl ANG/EP BN16 .....35 E1
Blenheim Dr ANG/EP BN16 .....35 E1
Blenheim Rd LAN/SOMP BN15 .....30 C5
Bluebell Dr ANG/EP BN16 .....35 E1
Blueberry Hl PUL/STOR RH20 .....11 G3
Blue Cedars Pl ANG/EP BN16 .....24 C3
Bodiam Av FERR BN12 .....37 H2
Bodmin Cl SALV BN13 .....27 G1
Bodmin Rd SALV BN13 .....27 G1
Bolsover Rd SALV BN13 .....38 D1
Bond St ARUN BN18 .....21 F3
The Bostal STEY/UB BN44 .....15 G5
Bostal Rd STEY/UB BN44 .....14 A4
Bost Hl FIN/BW BN14 .....19 H3
Botany Cl FERR BN12 .....35 G4
The Boulevard SALV BN13 .....27 G4
Boundary Cl WTHG BN11 .....2 A6
Boundary Rd LAN/SOMP BN15 .....30 D4
   WTHG BN11 .....39 F3
Boundary Wy ANG/EP BN16 .....36 C2
Boundstone Cl LAN/SOMP BN15 .....30 C2
Boundstone La
   LAN/SOMP BN15 .....30 B3
Bourne Cl SALV BN13 .....27 E3
Bower La PUL/STOR RH20 .....6 C3

Bowmans Cl STEY/UB BN44 .....14 C1
Bowness Av LAN/SOMP BN15 .....30 B4
Boxgrove FERR BN12 .....27 E5
Boxgrove Cl ANG/EP BN16 .....31 E1
Box Tree Av ANG/EP BN16 .....35 F1
Bracken Cl PUL/STOR RH20 .....11 G2
Bracken La PUL/STOR RH20 .....11 F2
Bramber Av PUL/STOR RH20 .....10 D2
Bramber Cl LAN/SOMP BN15 .....30 C1
Bramber Rd FIN/BW BN14 .....29 F2
   STEY/UB BN44 .....14 C3
Bramble Cl SALV BN13 .....27 G1
Bramble Crs SALV BN13 .....27 G1
Bramble La PUL/STOR * RH20 .....7 G2
   SALV BN13 .....27 G2
Brambletyne Cl SALV BN13 .....27 G3
The Bramblings ANG/EP BN16 .....35 G3
Bramley Cl FIN/BW BN14 .....29 E2
Bramley Rd FIN/BW BN14 .....29 E3
Breach Cl STEY/UB BN44 .....14 C3
Brecon Cl SALV BN13 .....28 A2
Brendon Rd SALV BN13 .....27 H1
Brendon Wy ANG/EP BN16 .....35 G2
Brewers Yd PUL/STOR RH20 .....10 C2
Brewery Hl ARUN BN18 .....21 G3
Briar Cl ANG/EP BN16 .....25 E5
Bridge Cl FERR BN12 .....38 B1
   LAN/SOMP BN15 .....30 D4
Bridge Rd FIN/BW BN14 .....29 F2
   LHPTN BN17 .....33 G3
Bridgnorth Cl SALV BN13 .....27 E4
Bridle Cl STEY/UB BN44 .....15 G3
Brierley Gdns LAN/SOMP BN15 .....31 E3
Brighton Rd HFD BN5 .....9 H4
   LAN/SOMP BN15 .....31 E5
   WTHG BN11 .....3 G5
Brisbane Cl SALV BN13 .....27 G3
Bristol Av LAN/SOMP BN15 .....31 G4
Brittany Rd FIN/BW BN14 .....28 D5
Broadmark Av ANG/EP BN16 .....35 F3
Broadmark La ANG/EP BN16 .....35 F3
Broadmark Pde ANG/EP * BN16 .....35 F3
Broadmark Wy ANG/EP BN16 .....35 F4
Broad Piece LHPTN BN17 .....33 G2
Broad Strd ANG/EP BN16 .....35 G5
Broadview Gdns SALV BN13 .....27 H1
Broadwater Bvd FIN/BW BN14 .....28 D4
Broadwater Hall FIN/BW * BN14 .....2 C1
Broadwater Ms FIN/BW * BN14 .....29 E4
Broadwater Rd FIN/BW BN14 .....29 E5
Broadwater St East
   FIN/BW BN14 .....29 E4
Broadwater St West
   FIN/BW BN14 .....28 D3
Broadwater Wy FIN/BW BN14 .....29 E4
The Broadway LAN/SOMP BN15 .....31 G4
Brockley Cl FIN/BW BN14 .....2 C1
Brook Barn Wy FERR BN12 .....38 D3
Brook Cha PUL/STOR * RH20 .....6 B3
Brook Cl PUL/STOR RH20 .....11 E1
   WTHG BN11 .....39 H5
Brookdean Rd WTHG BN11 .....41 E1
Brookenbee Cl ANG/EP BN16 .....35 E1
Brook La PUL/STOR RH20 .....24 A5
   FERR BN12 .....38 B1
Brooklyn Av WTHG BN11 .....39 E2
Brooklyn Chambers
   WTHG * BN11 .....39 E2
Brookpits La LHPTN BN17 .....32 D4
Brookside Av ANG/EP BN16 .....35 F1
Brookside Cl FERR BN12 .....37 E4
Brookside Rd ANG/EP BN16 .....37 E4
Brooks Wy PUL/STOR RH20 .....4 D3
Brook Wy LAN/SOMP BN15 .....31 E4
Broomers Hill La
   PUL/STOR RH20 .....5 F2
Broomers Hill Pk
   PUL/STOR * RH20 .....5 E1
Broomfield Av FIN/BW BN14 .....28 C4
Broomfield Rd HFD BN5 .....9 F3
Brou Cl ANG/EP BN16 .....36 C3
Brow Cl PUL/STOR RH20 .....10 A3
Browning Rd LAN/SOMP BN15 .....30 D1
   .....2 B3
Brown's La PUL/STOR RH20 .....10 C3
Bruce Av WTHG BN11 .....39 E1
Bruce Vls WTHG * BN11 .....39 E1
Bruce Wy WTHG BN11 .....39 E1
Brunswick Rd WTHG BN11 .....2 C1
Buckingham Rd WTHG BN11 .....2 E5
Buckwish La HFD BN5 .....9 H4
Bulkington Av WTHG BN11 .....2 B1
Bunbury Cl PUL/STOR RH20 .....11 G2
The Burchens FIN/BW * BN14 .....28 D3
Burford Cl SALV BN13 .....28 B2
Burley Cl LAN/SOMP * BN15 .....30 D3

Burlington Rd *FERR* BN12 ....38 C1
Burmill Ct *ANG/EP* BN16 ....35 H1
Burnham Rd *SALV* BN13 ....27 H3
Burnside Crs *LAN/SOMP* BN15....30 B4
Burrell Av *LAN/SOMP* BN15 ....30 C4
Burrell Buildings
　LAN/SOMP * BN15 ....30 C4
Burwash Cl *ANG/EP* BN16 ....36 C1
Bury Dr *FERR* BN12 ....38 A2
Bushby Av *ANG/EP* BN16 ....35 G5
Bushby Cl *LAN/SOMP* BN15 ....30 B4
Busticle La *LAN/SOMP* BN15 ....30 B2
Butler Ct *SALV* BN13 ....28 A3
Buttermere Wy *ANG/EP* BN16....34 D2
Byne Cl *PUL/STOR* RH20 ....10 D3
Byron Rd *ANG/EP* BN16 ....34 D3
　WTHG BN11 ....2 C5

C

Cagefoot La *HFD* BN5.........................9 G4
Caledonian Pl *WTHG* * BN11 ....2 E6
Callon Cl *SALV* * BN13 ....27 E3
Cambridge Rd *WTHG* BN11 ....2 D3
Camelia Cl *ANG/EP* BN16 ....34 D1
Campbell Ct *FERR* * BN12.............37 H1
Campbell Dr *ANG/EP* BN16...........35 E2
Canada Rd *ARUN* BN18 ....21 E3
Canberra Rd *SALV* BN13 ....27 F3
Canons Wy *STEY/UB* BN44 ....14 C1
Canterbury Ct *SALV* BN13............39 E1
Canterbury Rd *ANG/EP* BN16 .....35 G2
　SALV BN13 ....39 E1
The Cape *LHPTN* BN17 ....34 D3
Capstan Dr *ANG/EP* BN16............34 D2
Carisbrooke Cl *LAN/SOMP* BN15 ...30 D1
Carisbrooke Dr *SALV* BN13 ....27 E4
Carlton Ms *WTHG* BN11.................39 F3
Carnegie Cl *FERR* BN14.................28 D4
Carnegie Gdns *FIN/BW* BN14 .....28 D4
Carnegie Rd *FIN/BW* BN14 ....28 D4
Carnforth Rd *LAN/SOMP* BN15 ....30 A4
Caron Cl *LAN/SOMP* BN15 ....30 D4
Carpenters Meadow
　PUL/STOR * RH20 ....4 D4
Carvel Wy *PUL/STOR* RH20 ....34 D2
Cassidy Pl *PUL/STOR* RH20 ....10 A3
Castle Cl *SALV* BN13 ....28 A5
　STEY/UB BN44......................................14 D3
Castle Gdns *ARUN* * BN18 ....21 F3
Castle La *STEY/UB* BN44 ....14 D1
Castle Rd *SALV* BN13 ....28 A5
Castle Wy *SALV* BN13...................................28 A5
　STEY/UB BN44 ....14 D2
The Causeway *ARUN* BN18 ....21 H4
　FERR BN12 ....38 C1
Cavendish Cl *FERR* BN12..............38 C1
Cavendish Ms *WTHG* * BN11 ....2 C6
Cecilian Av *FIN/BW* BN14 ....29 E5
Cecil Pashley Wy *SHOR* BN43 ....31 H2
Cecil Rd *LAN/SOMP* BN15 ....30 D5
Cedar Av *SALV* BN13 ....28 A3
Cedar Cl *FERR* BN12 ....37 F3
　LAN/SOMP BN15 ....30 C5
　SALV BN13 ....28 A3
Cedar Ldg *ANG/EP* * BN16...........35 F3
The Cedars *ANG/EP* BN16............35 H2
Cedar Wy *HFD* BN5 ....9 H4
Central Av *ANG/EP* BN16 ....35 F4
　FIN/BW BN14.......................................20 A3
Centrecourt La *FIN/BW* BN14......2 D1
Centrecourt Rd *FIN/BW* BN14 ......2 D1
Chaffinch Cl *SALV* BN13................27 F4
Chalet Cl *FERR* BN12 ....37 F4
Chalet Gdns *FERR* BN12 ....37 G4
Chalet Rd *FERR* BN12 ....37 F3
Chalfont Wy *SALV* BN13 ....27 G4
Chanctonbury *PUL/STOR* RH20....8 C4
Chanctonbury Rd *ANG/EP* BN16...35 E4
Chanctonbury Vw *HFD* BN5 ....9 F3
Chanctonbury Wk
　PUL/STOR * RH20 ....10 C3
Chancton Cl *PUL/STOR* RH20 ......11 C1
　WTHG BN11 ....39 E1
Chancton Copse
　PUL/STOR * RH20 ....11 G1
Chancton View Rd *WTHG* BN11 ...39 E1
Chandlers Wy *STEY/UB* BN44 .....14 B2
Chandos Rd *WTHG* BN11 ....2 E6
Channel Keep *LHPTN* * BN17 ......34 B4
Chantry Cl *HFD* BN5 ....9 G2
　PUL/STOR RH20 ....10 D3
Chantryfield Rd *ANG/EP* BN16 ...25 E3
Chantry Rd *SALV* BN13 ....28 B3
Chapel Cl *LHPTN* BN17 ....33 H2

Chapel Rd *WTHG* BN11 ....2 E3
Chappell Cft *WTHG* * BN11 ....2 B4
Charlecote Rd *WTHG* BN11 ....3 G4
Charlton St *STEY/UB* BN44..........14 B2
Charmandean La *FIN/BW* BN14 ...29 E1
Charmandean Rd *FIN/BW* BN14 ...29 E3
Chartwell Rd *LAN/SOMP* BN15 ...30 C4
The Chase *FIN/BW* BN14................19 H1
Chatham Rd *WTHG* BN11 ....40 D1
Chatsmore Crs *FERR* BN12 ....37 H1
Chatsworth Cl *ANG/EP* BN16 ......35 E4
Chatsworth Dr *ANG/EP* BN16 .....35 E1
Chatsworth Rd *WTHG* BN11..........3 F5
Chaucer Rd *WTHG* BN11 ....2 B3
Chaucher Av *ANG/EP* BN16 ....35 E3
Cheam Rd *ANG/EP* BN16...............35 G4
Chelwood Av *FERR* BN12..............38 B3
Cherry Cft *LHPTN* BN17 ....34 A1
Cherry Gdns *SALV* BN13 ....19 H5
Cherry Tree Cl *SALV* BN13 ....19 G5
Cherry Wk *SALV* BN13 ....19 H5
Cherwell Rd *SALV* BN13 ....27 F1
Chesham Cl *FERR* BN12 ....38 D2
Chesley Cl *SALV* BN13...................27 F3
Chess Brook Gn *HFD* BN5 ....9 H2
Chesswood Av *WTHG* BN11 ....3 K1
Chesswood Rd *WTHG* BN11 ....3 H2
Chester Av *LAN/SOMP* BN15 ....30 D5
　WTHG BN11 ....3 K2
Chesterfield Rd *FERR* BN12 ....38 C1
Chestnut Cl *ANG/EP* * BN16 ....25 E5
　PUL/STOR RH20 ....11 C1
Chestnut Ct *ANG/EP* BN16 ....36 B3
Chestnut Rdg *PUL/STOR* RH20 .....6 B2
Chestnut Wk *FERR* BN12 ....27 E5
　PUL/STOR RH20 ....4 C4
Chestnut Wy *HFD* BN5 ....9 G3
Cheviot Cl *ANG/EP* BN16 ....36 B2
　SALV BN13 ....27 H1
Cheviot Rd *SALV* BN13 ....27 H1
Chichester Ct *WTHG* * BN11 ....39 F3
Chilgrove Cl *FERR* BN12 ....38 A1
Chiltern Cl *ANG/EP* BN16 ....36 B2
Chiltern Crs *SALV* BN13 ....27 H1
Chiltington Cl *PUL/STOR* RH20 ....6 B3
The Chine *LHPTN* BN17 ....34 D4
Chippers Cl *SALV* BN13..................28 A5
Chippers Rd *SALV* BN13 ....28 A5
Chippers Wk *SALV* * BN13 ....28 A5
Christchurch Rd *WTHG* BN11 ....2 E3
Church Ap *LHPTN* BN17 ....34 B4
Church Cl *LAN/SOMP* BN15 ....30 D1
　PUL/STOR RH20 ....8 B4
　SALV BN13 ....18 C5
　STEY/UB BN44 ....15 F2
Church Farm Wk *STEY/UB* BN44 ...15 F2
Church HI *PUL/STOR* RH20 ....4 C4
Churchill Pde *ANG/EP* * BN16 .....35 F5
Church La *FERR* BN12 ....37 F2
　HFD BN5...9 G3
　LAN/SOMP BN15 ....29 H2
　LHPTN BN17 ....22 D3
　LHPTN BN17 ....32 D3
　PUL/STOR RH20 ....8 B4
　STEY/UB BN44.....................................14 C2
　STEY/UB BN44 ....15 F3
Church Ms *STEY/UB* BN44 ....14 C1
Church Pl *PUL/STOR* RH20 ....4 C4
Church Rd *ANG/EP* BN16 ....25 E4
　ANG/EP BN16 ....35 F3
　LHPTN BN17 ....22 D3
　SALV BN13 ....28 B4
Church St *ARUN* BN18 ....12 B1
　HFD BN5...9 G3
　LHPTN BN17 ....34 B3
　PUL/STOR RH20 ....10 C3
　STEY/UB BN44.....................................14 C2
Church Wk *WTHG* BN11 ....3 K4
Church Wy *SALV* BN13...................28 A4
Church Way Cl *SALV* BN13 ....28 A4
Chute Av *SALV* BN13 ....19 H5
Chute Wy *SALV* BN13.....................27 H1
The Circle *ANG/EP* BN16 ....36 B4
Cissbury Av *FIN/BW* BN14 ....20 A4
Cissbury Dr *FIN/BW* BN14............20 A3
Cissbury Gdns *FIN/BW* BN14 ......20 B3
Cissbury Rd *FERR* BN12.................37 F1
　FIN/BW BN14 ....28 D3
Claigmar Rd *ANG/EP* BN16 ....35 F3
Clapham Cl *SALV* BN13..................18 C5
Clapham Common *SALV* BN13 ....26 B1
Clare Ldg *ANG/EP* * BN16.............35 E3
Clarence Av *LHPTN* BN17 ....33 H1
Clarence Dr *ANG/EP* BN16............36 A2
Clarence Ter *HFD* * BN5 ....9 G4
Clarendon Rd *FIN/BW* BN14.........29 F3
Clays HI *STEY/UB* BN44.................14 D3
Cleeves Wy *ANG/EP* BN16 ....35 G2

Cleveland Cl *SALV* BN13 ....28 A1
Cleveland Rd *SALV* BN13..............28 A1
Clifton Ct *WTHG* * BN11 ....2 D3
Clifton Gdns *WTHG* * BN11 ....2 D3
Clifton Rd *LHPTN* BN17 ....34 A4
　WTHG BN11 ....2 D3
Climping Pk *LHPTN* * BN17..........33 E4
Climping St *LHPTN* BN17 ....32 C4
Clive Av *FERR* BN12 ....38 C2
Clivedale Gdns *STEY/UB* BN44....14 C2
The Cloisters *LHPTN* BN17 ....34 C4
The Close *ANG/EP* BN16 ....35 G4
　LAN/SOMP BN15 ....31 E5
　PUL/STOR RH20 ....8 C3
Clover La *FERR* BN12 ....37 F3
Club Wk *ANG/EP* BN16 ....36 B4
Clun Rd *LHPTN* BN17 ....33 G1
Clyde Cl *SALV* BN13 ....27 F1
Clyde Rd *SALV* BN13.......................27 F2
Clyde Ter *STEY/UB* * BN44 ....14 D2
Coach House Ms *WTHG* BN11 ....2 D5
Coastal Rd *FERR* BN12...................38 A5
Coastguard Rd *LHPTN* BN17 ....34 A5
Cobden Rd *WTHG* BN11...................2 C4
Cokeham Gdns
　LAN/SOMP BN15 ....30 B3
Cokeham La *LAN/SOMP* BN15.....30 B3
Cokeham Rd *LAN/SOMP* BN15....30 B2
Coldharbour La *SALV* BN13 ....18 A5
Colebrook Cl *WTHG* BN11 ....3 K2
Colebrook Rd *LHPTN* BN17 ....34 A1
Coleridge Cl *FERR* BN12................38 A1
Coleridge Crs *FERR* BN12.............37 H1
Coleridge Rd *FERR* BN12 ....38 A1
Colindale Rd *FERR* BN12 ....37 F2
Colindale Rd North *FERR* BN12 ...37 F2
College Gdns *WTHG* BN11 ....39 F2
College HI *STEY/UB* BN44 ....14 C3
College Rd *STEY/UB* BN44 ....15 H4
Collingwood *PUL/STOR* RH20 ....4 D3
Collingwood Rd *FERR* BN12 ....27 F5
Colne Cl *SALV* BN13 ....27 F1
Columbia Dr *SALV* BN13 ....27 F3
Columbine Wy *ANG/EP* BN16 ......35 E1
Combe Dr *STEY/UB* BN44..............14 C4
Commerce Wy *LAN/SOMP* BN15 ...30 B4
The Common *PUL/STOR* RH20.......6 B1
Common HI *PUL/STOR* RH20 ....6 B2
Compass Cl *LHPTN* BN17 ....34 D2
Compton Av *FERR* BN12................38 A2
Conbar Av *ANG/EP* BN16 ....35 F2
Concorde Cl *PUL/STOR* RH20 ......11 E1
Congreve Rd *FIN/BW* BN14...........29 F5
Coniston Cl *LAN/SOMP* BN15.......30 B3
Coniston Rd *FERR* BN12 ....27 F5
Coniston Wy *ANG/EP* BN16..........34 D1
Connaught Rd *LHPTN* BN17 ....34 A4
Convent Gdns *FIN/BW* BN14........13 H5
Coombe Dro *STEY/UB* BN44 ....14 B3
Coombelands La *PUL/STOR* RH20 ...4 B3
Coombe Ri *FIN/BW* BN14 ....20 B4
Coombe Rd *STEY/UB* BN44 ....14 B3
Coombes Wy *LHPTN* BN17 ....23 E5
Coopers Wy *HFD* BN5......................9 H3
Cootham Gdns *PUL/STOR* RH20 ...10 A2
Copper Hall Cl *ANG/EP* * BN16....35 H2
Coppetts Wd *ANG/EP* * BN16 ......35 E4
Copse Vw *ANG/EP* BN16 ....36 A2
Copthorne Cl *SALV* BN13...............28 B2
Copthorne HI *SALV* BN13 ....28 A2
Cordal Cl *ANG/EP* BN16.................35 E5
Corfe Cl *SALV* BN13 ....27 E4
Corner Garth *FERR* BN12..............37 G3
Cornfield Cl *LHPTN* BN17..............34 B1
Cornwall Gdns *LHPTN* BN17.........34 A3
Cornwall Rd *LHPTN* BN17 ....34 A2
Cortis Av *FIN/BW* BN14 ....28 D4
Cote St *SALV* BN13 ....19 F5
Cotswold Cl *SALV* BN13.................27 H1
Cotswold Rd *SALV* BN13................27 H1
Cotswold Wy *ANG/EP* BN16 ....36 B2
Cottenham Rd *WTHG* BN11 ....3 J2
The Cottrells *ANG/EP* BN16 ....25 E4
Countryside Farm Pk
　STEY/UB * BN44 ....15 F2
Courtfields *LAN/SOMP* * BN15....30 C4
Courtlands Cl *FERR* BN12 ....38 D3
Courtlands Wy *FERR* BN12 ....38 D3
Courtwick La *LHPTN* BN17 ....22 D5
Courtwick Rd *LHPTN* BN17 ....33 H1
The Courtyard *WTHG* * BN11 ....2 A3
Cousins Wy *PUL/STOR* RH20 ....4 D3
Coventry Ct *WTHG* * BN11 ....39 F2
Cove Rd *ANG/EP* BN16 ....35 E4
Covert Md *PUL/STOR* RH20............4 C4
Cowdray Cl *ANG/EP* BN16 ....35 E1
　FERR BN12...38 C3
Cowdray Ct *FERR* * BN12 ....38 A4

Cowdray Dr *ANG/EP* BN16 3
　FERR BN12...3
Cowley Dr *LAN/SOMP* BN15 3
Cowper Rd *WTHG* BN11 3
Coxham La *STEY/UB* BN44 1
Crabtree Ar *LAN/SOMP* * BN15 3
Crabtree La *LAN/SOMP* BN15.......3
Cradock Pl *SALV* BN13...................3
Craggits La *HFD* BN5 3
Cranleigh Rd *FIN/BW* BN14 2
Cranmer Rd *SALV* BN13.................3
Cranworth Rd *WTHG* BN11 3
Cray La *PUL/STOR* RH20 3
Cray's La *PUL/STOR* RH20 3
The Crescent *ANG/EP* BN16 3
　ANG/EP * BN16 3
　LAN/SOMP BN15 3
　STEY/UB BN44 1
Crescent Ri *PUL/STOR* RH20.........1
Crescent Rd *WTHG* BN11 3
Cricketers Cl *PUL/STOR* RH20 1
Cricketers Pde *FIN/BW* * BN14 2
Cripps La *STEY/UB* BN44...............1
Crockhurst HI *SALV* BN13 2
The Croft *ANG/EP* BN16.................3
Crofters Wd *STEY/UB* BN44 1
Croft La *HFD* BN5............................
Croft Vis *HFD* * BN5........................
Crookthorn La *LHPTN* BN17..........3
Crosby Cl *SALV* BN13 3
Croshaw Cl *LAN/SOMP* BN15 3
Cross La *FIN/BW* BN14 3
Cross Rd *ANG/EP* BN16..................3
Cross St *WTHG* BN11......................3
The Crossways *LHPTN* BN17 3
Crossways *ANG/EP* BN16 3
　PUL/STOR RH20 2
Crossways Av *FERR* BN12 2
Crossways Pk *PUL/STOR* RH20 3
Crouch HI *HFD* BN5 3
Crowborough Dr *FERR* BN12.........3
Crown Buildings
　LAN/SOMP * BN15 3
Crundens Cnr *ANG/EP* BN16 3
Cuckfield Crs *SALV* BN13...............2
Cudlow Av *ANG/EP* BN16 3
Cudlow Gdn *ANG/EP* BN16............3
Culver Rd *LAN/SOMP* BN15 3
Cumberland Av *FERR* BN12 3
Cumberland Crs *ANG/EP* BN16 2
Cumberland Rd *ANG/EP* BN16......2
Cumbrian Cl *SALV* BN13 2
Curvins Wy *LAN/SOMP* BN15 3
Curzon Cl *SALV* BN13.....................3
Cypress Av *SALV* BN13 2
Cyprus Vis *LHPTN* BN17 33

D

Dagbrook La *HFD* BN5 ....
Dagmar St *WTHG* BN11..................3
The Daisycroft *HFD* BN5.................
Dale Rd *WTHG* BN11.......................30
Daltons Pl *ARUN* BN18 30
Daniel Cl *LAN/SOMP* BN15 3
Dankton Gdns *LAN/SOMP* BN15 ...30
Dankton La *LAN/SOMP* BN15........30
Dapper's La *ANG/EP* BN16 2
Dart Cl *SALV* BN13 3
Davits Dr *LHPTN* BN17 34
Dawes Av *WTHG* BN11...................3
Dawes Cl *WTHG* BN11 30
Dawn Cl *STEY/UB* BN44 15
Dawn Crs *STEY/UB* BN44 15
Dawtrey Cl *ANG/EP* BN16 3
Deacons Wy *STEY/UB* BN44.........15
Deacon Wy *FIN/BW* BN14.............3
Dean Cl *LHPTN* BN17.....................3
Dean Wy *PUL/STOR* RH20 10
De Braose Wy *STEY/UB* BN44 14
Decoy Dr *ANG/EP* BN16 20
Decoy La *ANG/EP* BN16 20
Decoy Rd *FIN/BW* BN14 20
Deer Pk *HFD* BN5 ....
Deerswood Cl *SALV* BN13..............25
Dell Dr *ANG/EP* BN16.....................
The Deneway *LAN/SOMP* BN15.....30
Denshire Dr *PUL/STOR* RH20........10
Denton Cl *FERR* BN12....................38
Derek Rd *LAN/SOMP* BN15 30
　LAN/SOMP BN15 30
Derwent Cl *ANG/EP* BN16..............30
Derwent Dr *FERR* BN12 27
Devonport Pl *WTHG* BN11.............40
Devonport Rd *WTHG* BN11 40
Dingley Rd *ANG/EP* BN16..............16

ale Gdns *ANG/EP* BN16 ....35 F2
ling Cl *FERR* BN12.................27 E5
.a *STEY/UB* BN44................14 C2
nin Wy *ANG/EP* BN16 ....35 G4
nion Buildings
/BW * BN14..........................29 G5
nion Cl *FIN/BW* BN14............29 F5
nion Rd *FIN/BW* BN14............29 F5
nion Wy *ANG/EP* BN16 ....35 F1
/BW BN14.............................29 G4
nion Wy West
ington Pl *ANG/EP * BN16 .....35 F2
e End *FERR* BN12.................37 G4
ester Gdns *WTHG* BN11 ....39 F2
et Cl *LHPTN* BN17...............34 B3
et Pl *SALV* * BN13................28 B4
alas M *WTHG* BN11..............39 E2
alas Cl *ARUN* BN18...............32 A2
HG BN11...............................39 E2
cote Ms *LAN/SOMP* BN15 ...30 B1
r Rd *WTHG* BN11.................39 F3
nland Cl *FIN/BW* BN14...........13 H5
EY/UB BN44...........................15 G3
nland Rd *STEY/UB* BN44........15 G3
nlands *PUL/STOR* RH20 ....5 E4
nlands Av *ANG/EP* BN16 ....29 E2
nlands Cl *LAN/SOMP* BN15...30 B2
nlands Gdns *FIN/BW* BN14.....29 F5
nlands Pde *FIN/BW * BN14 ....29 F2
ns Cl *LAN/SOMP* BN15...........31 G3
nscroft *STEY/UB* BN44 ....15 G4
nside Av *FIN/BW* BN14...........19 H3
nside Cl *FIN/BW* BN14...........19 H3
ns Link *STEY/UB* BN44...........15 F5
ns Md *LAN/SOMP* * BN15 .....30 B1
nsview Av *PUL/STOR* RH20 ...10 D2
nsview Rd *ANG/EP* BN16 ......37 E4
ns Wy *ANG/EP* BN16.............36 A1
nview *FERR* BN12.................37 F1
nview Rd *FERR* BN12............37 F1
/BW BN14..............................13 H4
n View Rd *WTHG* BN11 ....39 F1
e Av *FERR* BN12...................27 G5
e Gv *ARUN* BN18..................32 A2
es Cl *LAN/SOMP* BN15...........31 G3
cliff Cl *FERR* BN12................37 F3
vetts Cl *ANG/EP* BN16 ....35 E1
Driftway *ANG/EP* BN16..........35 E1
EY/UB BN44...........................15 G2
Drills *ANG/EP * BN16 ....29 E4
Drive *ANG/EP* BN16...............36 C4
N/SOMP BN15........................30 C5
HG BN11...............................39 E1
ping Holms *HFD* BN5..............9 F4
nmond Ct *FERR* * BN12.........38 C3
nmond Rd *FERR* BN12...........38 D3
es Cl *ARUN* BN18..................21 E3
e's Hl *PUL/STOR* RH20 ....7 F1
e St *LHPTN* BN17.................34 A3
es Yd *STEY/UB* BN44............14 C2
cton Rd *ANG/EP* BN16 ....35 F2
ington Gdns *FERR* * BN12 .....38 C1
ington Hl *SALV* BN13............27 G2
ington La *SALV* BN13............27 G3

E

es Cha *LHPTN* BN17..............22 D5
Av *FERR* BN12......................39 E3
court Rd *FIN/BW* BN14...........2 D1
Court Wy *ANG/EP* BN16........35 G2
Dr *ANG/EP* BN16.................24 D5
ergate Cl *FERR* BN12............37 G2
ern Cl *ANG/EP* BN16.............36 C2
Ham Rd *LHPTN* BN17............33 H3
ing Cl *FIN/BW* BN14..............29 G4
Md *FERR* BN12....................37 G3
Onslow Cl *FERR* BN12..........37 F2
St *ARUN* BN18.....................12 C1
N/SOMP BN15........................30 D5
PTN BN17..............................34 B3
Tyne *SALV* BN13.................27 G3
ehill Cl *SALV* BN13................28 A2
onton Rd *SALV* BN13............27 F3
ards Ter *LAN/SOMP* * BN15 ...29 G2
ards Wy *LHPTN* BN17...........22 D5
in Cl *LAN/SOMP* BN15...........30 B3
ath Av *LAN/SOMP* BN15.......30 D2
ne Av *FERR* BN12.................39 E3
ne Rd *FERR* BN12.................38 D3
n Rd *WTHG* BN11................3 J3
n Wy *LHPTN* BN17...............33 C2
n Rd *FERR* BN12.................38 C2
abeth Pl *LAN/SOMP* BN15 ....30 B4
abeth Rd *WTHG* BN11...........2 D4

Ellis Av *SALV* BN13................27 H1
Ellis Cl *ARUN* BN18...............21 E4
Elm Av *ANG/EP* BN16............36 B3
Elm Gv *LAN/SOMP* BN15.......30 C4
WTHG BN11...........................39 E1
Elm Grove La *STEY/UB* BN44 .14 C2
Elmgrove Rd *LHPTN* BN17 .....34 B2
Elmhurst Cl *LHPTN* BN17.......25 F3
Elm Pk *FERR* BN12................37 G1
Elm Pl *ANG/EP* BN16.............35 G3
Elm Ri *FIN/BW* BN14.............13 H5
Elm Rd *WTHG* BN11..............3 C5
Elms Dr *LAN/SOMP* BN15......30 C3
Elmstone Cl *LAN/SOMP* BN15 .30 C3
Elsie Rd *WTHG* BN11..............2 B6
Elverlands Cl *FERR* BN12........37 G4
Ely Cl *SALV* BN13..................28 A5
Ely Rd *SALV* BN13.................28 A5
Ennerdale Dr *LAN/SOMP* BN15 .30 A4
Ensign Wy *ANG/EP* BN16........34 D2
Enterprise Ct *FERR* * BN12......38 D1
Eriskay Ct *SALV* BN13............27 E3
Eriswell Rd *WTHG* BN11.........2 A1
The Esplanade *WTHG* BN11.....3 J5
Esplanade Ct *WTHG* * BN11.....3 K5
Essenhigh Dr *SALV* BN13.........27 E3
The Estuary *LHPTN* BN17........34 C3
Ethelred Rd *SALV* BN13..........28 B5
Ethelwulf Rd *SALV* BN13.........28 B5
Eton Rd *WTHG* BN11..............39 F1
Evelyn Av *ANG/EP* BN16........35 G4
Evelyn Rd *FIN/BW* BN14........39 F3
Exeter Ct *WTHG* * BN11.........39 F3
Exmoor Cl *SALV* BN13............27 G2
Exmoor Crs *SALV* BN13..........27 H2
Exmoor Dr *SALV* BN13...........27 H1

F

Fabians Wy *HFD* BN5.............9 F4
Faircox La *HFD* BN5...............9 G4
Fairfield Ms *PUL/STOR* * RH20 ...8 B4
Fairfield Rd *PUL/STOR* RH20 ....8 C4
Fairfields *SALV* BN13.............28 B4
Fairfield Wy *PUL/STOR* RH20....8 C4
Fairlands *ANG/EP* BN16..........36 A3
Fairlawn *ANG/EP* BN16..........35 F2
Fairlawn Dr *FIN/BW* BN14......29 E5
Fairlead *LHPTN* BN17.............34 C3
Fairview Av *FERR* BN12..........38 B3
Fairview Rd *LAN/SOMP* BN15 ..30 D1
The Fairway *LAN/SOMP* BN15 ..31 F4
Fairway *LHPTN* BN17.............34 C4
Faithfull Crs *PUL/STOR* RH20 ..10 A2
Falcon Gdns *LHPTN* BN17.......22 D5
Falkland Av *LHPTN* BN17........34 C2
Falmer Av *FERR* BN12............38 A3
Falmer Cl *FERR* BN12............38 B3
Faraday Cl *SALV* BN13............27 F3
Farm Acre *ANG/EP* * BN16 .....36 A2
Farm Cl *HFD* BN5..................9 C3
Farm Wy *ANG/EP* BN16.........35 E3
Farncombe Rd *WTHG* BN11.....3 J3
Farnfold Rd *STEY/UB* BN44.....14 C1
The Faroes *LHPTN* BN17.........34 D1
Fastnet Wy *LHPTN* BN17........34 D3
Fawn Ri *HFD* BN5..................9 G2
Fereday Cl *LAN/SOMP* BN15 ...30 D3
Ferndale Wk *ANG/EP* BN16.....25 F3
Fernhurst Dr *FERR* BN12........37 H2
Fern Rd *PUL/STOR* RH20........10 D3
Ferring Grange Gdns
FERR BN12...........................37 F2
Ferringham La *FERR* BN12.......37 F3
Ferringham Wy *FERR* BN12......37 F4
Ferring La *FERR* BN12.............37 G4
Ferring Marine *FERR* BN12 .....37 G4
Ferring St *FERR* BN12.............37 F2
Ferry Rd *LHPTN* BN17............33 G4
Fetherston Rd *LAN/SOMP* BN15 .30 C2
Field Cl *LAN/SOMP* BN15........30 C3
Field End *PUL/STOR* RH20 ......10 D3
Field Pl *LHPTN* BN17..............34 A3
Field Place Pde *FERR* * BN12....38 D1
Field Rw *WTHG* BN11.............2 E5
Fifth Av *FIN/BW* BN14...........28 D1
LAN/SOMP BN15...................30 D2
Fincham Cl *ANG/EP* BN16.......36 A3
Finches Cl *LAN/SOMP* BN15 ....30 C4
LHPTN BN17........................22 D5
Finches La *PUL/STOR* RH20 .....6 B1
Findon By-Pass *FIN/BW* BN14 ...13 G5
Findon Rd *FIN/BW* BN14.........20 A2

Finisterre Wy *LHPTN* BN17......34 D4
Fircroft Av *LAN/SOMP* BN15 ...30 C1
Fircroft Crs *ANG/EP* BN16.......35 G2
Firsdown Cl *SALV* BN13..........19 H4
Firsdown Rd *SALV* BN13.........19 H4
First Av *FIN/BW* BN14...........28 D1
LAN/SOMP BN15...................30 D1
Fir Tree Cl *PUL/STOR* RH20......6 C3
Fir Tree La *PUL/STOR* RH20......6 C3
Fishers Cl *ANG/EP* BN16.........34 D4
Fittleworth Cl *FERR* BN12.......26 D5
Fitzalan Rd *ARUN* BN18..........21 F5
LHPTN BN17........................34 B4
Fleet Cl *LHPTN* BN17.............34 D2
Fletcher Rd *FIN/BW* BN14.......29 F4
Fletcher Wy *ANG/EP* BN16......25 E3
Flint Cl *ANG/EP* BN16............36 A2
The Florets *STEY/UB* * BN44.....15 C4
Florida Cl *FERR* BN12.............37 G4
Florida Gdns *FERR* BN12.........37 G4
Florida Rd *FERR* BN12............37 G4
Florlandia Cl *LAN/SOMP* BN15 .30 A4
Flower Farm Cl *HFD* BN5........9 F3
Foamcourt Waye *FERR* BN12 ...37 F3
Fontwell Rd *ANG/EP* BN16......35 E4
FIN/BW BN14.......................28 B1
Ford Rd *ARUN* BN18..............32 D1
Fordwater Gdns *ARUN* BN18....32 A1
Forest Rd *FIN/BW* BN14.........29 E3
Forge Cl *ANG/EP* BN16...........36 A2
Forsters Yd *LHPTN* * BN17......33 C3
Fort Rd *LHPTN* BN17.............33 H2
Foster La *PUL/STOR* RH20........8 B4
Fosters Cl *ANG/EP* BN16.........35 H4
Fourth Av *FIN/BW* BN14.........29 E2
LAN/SOMP BN15...................30 D2
Fox Ct *PUL/STOR* RH20..........10 A3
Foxdale Dr *ANG/EP* BN16........25 E5
Fox Dell *PUL/STOR* RH20........10 A3
Foxes Cl *ANG/EP* BN16...........24 A5
Foxfields *PUL/STOR* RH20........6 B1
Foxglove Wk *FERR* BN12.........27 F5
Foxglove Wy *ANG/EP* BN16.....34 D1
Fox Lea *FIN/BW* BN14...........19 H1
Foxley La *SALV* BN13.............28 A1
Frampton Ct *FERR* * BN12........38 B2
The Framptons *ANG/EP* BN16...36 C3
France La *SALV* BN13.............26 A1
Franciscan Wy *LHPTN* BN17.....34 A3
Franklands Cl *FIN/BW* BN14....20 A5
Franklin Rd *SALV* BN13..........27 H2
Frenches Rd *PUL/STOR* RH20 ..10 C2
Freshbrook Cl *LAN/SOMP* BN15 .30 D4
Freshbrook Rd *LAN/SOMP* BN15 .31 E4
Freshfields Cl *LAN/SOMP* BN15 .30 C3
Freshfields Dr *LAN/SOMP* BN15 .30 C3
Friar Wk *SALV* BN13.............39 H1
Frobisher Cl *FERR* BN12.........27 G5
Frobisher Wy *ANG/EP* BN16....35 H4
FERR BN12...........................27 G5
Fryern Cl *PUL/STOR* RH20 ......10 A3
Fryern Rd *PUL/STOR* RH20......10 C1
Fulbeck Av *SALV* BN13...........27 E3
Fullers Wk *LHPTN* BN17.........23 E4
The Furlongs *STEY/UB* BN44....14 C3
Furners Md *HFD* BN5.............9 H4
Furze Cl *SALV* BN13..............19 G4
Furze Common Rd
PUL/STOR RH20....................7 E3
Furzedown *LHPTN* BN17.........34 B4
Furzefield Cl *ANG/EP* BN16.....25 E2
Furzeholme *SALV* BN13..........19 H4
Furze Rd *SALV* BN13.............19 G4

G

The Gables *PUL/STOR* * RH20...10 D3
Gainsborough Av *FIN/BW* BN14 .29 E5
Gainsborough Ldg
FIN/BW * BN14....................28 D5
Gaisford Cl *FIN/BW* BN14.......2 C1
Gaisford Rd *FIN/BW* BN14......28 C5
Galsworthy Cl *FERR* BN12.......38 A1
Galsworthy Rd *FERR* BN12......38 A1
Ganders Cl *HFD* * BN5...........9 C3
Gannon Rd *WTHG* BN11.........3 K3
Garden Cl *ANG/EP* BN16.........25 F2
LAN/SOMP BN15...................30 B3
PUL/STOR RH20....................10 C2
Garden Wood Cl
PUL/STOR RH20....................6 C3
Garrick Rd *FIN/BW* BN14.......29 E5
Gatcombe Cl *SALV* * BN13......27 E4
Gatewycke Ter *STEY/UB* * BN44 .14 C2
Genoa *ANG/EP* BN16.............34 D2
Georges La *PUL/STOR* RH20....11 H3

George V Av *LAN/SOMP* BN15 ..31 G4
WTHG BN11.........................38 D1
Georgia Av *FIN/BW* BN14.......29 E5
Georgian Gdns *ANG/EP* BN16 ...35 H2
Gerald Rd *WTHG* BN11...........39 E3
The Gilberts *ANG/EP* BN16......35 E5
Gladonian Rd *LHPTN* BN17......34 A1
Gladstone Ter *LHPTN* BN17.....34 A1
Glebe Cl *LAN/SOMP* BN15.......30 D2
Glebelands *PUL/STOR* RH20.....5 E3
Glebe Rd *SALV* BN13..............28 B4
Glebeside Av *FIN/BW* BN14.....28 B4
Glebeside Cl *FIN/BW* BN14......28 B4
Glebe Wy *LAN/SOMP* BN15.....30 D2
Glenbarrie Wy *FERR* BN12......37 E1
The Glen *FERR* BN12..............28 B2
Glen Gdns *FERR* BN12............37 G2
Glenville Rd *ANG/EP* BN16......35 F4
Globe Pl *LHPTN* BN17............34 A1
Gloucester La *LHPTN* BN17......34 A3
Gloucester Pl *LHPTN* BN17......34 A3
Gloucester Rd *LHPTN* BN17.....33 H3
Glynde Av *FERR* BN12............37 G2
Glynde Cl *FERR* BN12.............37 G2
Goda Rd *LHPTN* BN17............34 B3
Godstalls La *STEY/UB* BN44.....14 B2
Goldcrest Av *LHPTN* BN17.......22 D5
Golden Acre *ANG/EP* BN16......36 C4
Golden Av *ANG/EP* BN16.........36 C4
Golden Avenue Cl *ANG/EP* BN16 .36 C4
Goldsmith Rd *FIN/BW* BN14....29 F5
Goodwood Cl *ANG/EP* BN16 ....35 H2
Goodwood Rd *SALV* BN13.......28 B2
Gordon Rd *LAN/SOMP* BN15 ...30 C3
WTHG BN11.........................3 F3
Goring Cha *FERR* BN12...........26 D5
Goring Rd *FERR* BN12.............38 B2
STEY/UB BN44......................14 C3
Goring St *FERR* BN12.............26 D5
Goring Wy *FERR* BN12............37 H2
Gorse Av *ANG/EP* BN16..........37 E5
FIN/BW BN14.......................28 C3
Gorse Bank Cl *PUL/STOR* RH20 .11 H1
Gorse La *SALV* BN13..............19 H4
Gorse Vw *ANG/EP* * BN16.......36 D4
Gosden Rd *LHPTN* BN17.........34 C2
Grafton Cl *ANG/EP* BN16.........35 F2
Grafton Dr *LAN/SOMP* BN15 ...30 B3
Grafton Gdns *LAN/SOMP* BN15 .30 B3
Grafton Pl *WTHG* BN11..........2 E5
Grafton Rd *WTHG* BN11.........2 E5
Graham Rd *WTHG* BN11.........2 E5
Granary Wy *LHPTN* BN17........23 E5
Grand Av *LAN/SOMP* BN15 .....30 D2
LHPTN BN17........................33 H1
WTHG BN11.........................39 F2
Grange Cl *FERR* BN12.............37 F3
Grange Ct *FERR* * BN12..........37 F2
Grange Park Rd *FERR* BN12.....37 F3
The Grangeway *ANG/EP* BN16 ..35 F3
Grantsmead *LAN/SOMP* BN15 ..30 D2
Granville Rd *LHPTN* BN17.......34 B4
Grasmere Av *LAN/SOMP* BN15 .30 A3
Grasmere Cl *LHPTN* BN17.......34 C3
Gratwicke Rd *WTHG* BN11......2 D5
Gravelly Crs *LAN/SOMP* BN15 ..31 E3
Greatham Rd *FIN/BW* BN14.....20 A5
Greenacre Cl *PUL/STOR* * RH20 .10 A3
Greenacres *PUL/STOR* RH20.....8 C2
STEY/UB BN44......................14 C3
Greenacres Ring *ANG/EP* BN16 .25 E3
Green Bushes Cl *ANG/EP* BN16 .35 E4
Greenfields *LHPTN* BN17.........33 G1
Greenfield Wy *PUL/STOR* RH20 .10 D2
Greenhurst La *PUL/STOR* RH20 .6 D4
Greenland Cl *SALV* BN13.........27 H2
Greenland Rd *SALV* BN13........27 H3
Green Lane Cl *ARUN* BN18......21 E4
Greenoaks *LAN/SOMP* BN15 ....30 C2
The Green *PUL/STOR* * RH20....4 D2
PUL/STOR RH20....................11 E2
Green Pk *FERR* BN12.............37 G1
Greentrees *LAN/SOMP* * BN15 ..30 B3
Greentrees Cl *LAN/SOMP* BN15 .30 B3
Greentrees Crs *LAN/SOMP* BN15 .30 B3
The Green Wy *FERR* BN12.......27 E5
Greenways Crs *FERR* BN12......37 G3
Greenwood Dr *ANG/EP* BN16 ...36 A1
Greet Rd *LAN/SOMP* BN15......30 C2
Grenville Av *FERR* BN12.........38 C1
Grenville Cl *FERR* BN12..........38 B1
Gresham Pl *HFD* BN5.............9 F2
Greyfriars Cl *SALV* BN13.........28 B3
Greyfriars La *PUL/STOR* RH20 ..10 B4
Greystoke Ms *LHPTN* BN17.....37 F2
Greystoke Rd *FERR* BN12........37 F2
Greystone Av *SALV* BN13........28 A4
Griffin Crs *LHPTN* BN17..........23 E5

Griffith's Av *LAN/SOMP* BN15 ....30 C1
Grinstead Av *LAN/SOMP* BN15 ....30 D3
Grinstead La *LAN/SOMP* BN15.......30 D3
Grosvenor Rd *WTHG* BN11 ....2 E4
The Grove *FERR* BN12.......................37 F2
Grove Crs *LHPTN* BN17 ....34 B2
The Grovelands
   LAN/SOMP BN15.........................30 D5
Grove La *PUL/STOR* RH20 ....6 C3
Grover Av *LAN/SOMP* BN15 ....30 C2
Grove Rd *FIN/BW* BN14.....................28 D3
Guernsey Rd *FERR* BN12....................37 G4
Guildford Cl *FIN/BW* BN14................28 B5
Guildford Rd *ANG/EP* BN16 ....35 H2
   FIN/BW BN14..............................39 F1

H

Hacketts La *HFD* * BN5 ....9 G3
Hadley Av *FIN/BW* BN14 ....29 E2
Hadlow Wy *LAN/SOMP* BN15.........31 D3
Haglands Copse *PUL/STOR* RH20 ....6 C2
Haglands La *PUL/STOR* RH20............6 C2
Haigh Cl *LAN/SOMP* BN15...............31 G3
Hailsham Cl *ANG/EP* BN16 ....36 C1
Hailsham Rd *WTHG* BN11 ....39 E3
Halewick Cl *LAN/SOMP* BN15..........30 B5
Halewick La *LAN/SOMP* BN15 ....30 B1
Half Moon La *SALV* BN13 ....28 A1
Half Moon Pde *SALV* * BN13............28 A2
Halifax Dr *SALV* BN13 ....27 F3
Hall Av *FIN/BW* BN14.......................28 B2
Hall Cl *FIN/BW* BN14.......................28 B2
Halsbury Cl *WTHG* BN11....................3 H2
Halsbury Rd *WTHG* BN11 ....3 J2
Hamble Gdns *SALV* BN13 ....27 F2
Hamble Rd *LAN/SOMP* BN15 ....30 A3
Hamble Wy *SALV* BN13 ....28 A1
Ham Cl *FIN/BW* BN14.......................29 H5
Hamilton Cl *ANG/EP* BN16 ....35 E1
   FIN/BW BN14..............................29 F4
Hamilton Ct *FERR* * BN12 ....27 G5
Hamilton Dr *ANG/EP* BN16 ....35 E1
Hamilton Ms *LAN/SOMP* * BN15 ....30 B2
Hamilton Rd *LAN/SOMP* BN15........30 C2
Ham Manor Cl *ANG/EP* BN16 ....24 C5
Ham Manor Wy *ANG/EP* BN16.........24 D5
Hammond Dr *SALV* BN13 ....27 G1
Hammond Pl *PUL/STOR* * RH20.......10 C3
Hampers La *PUL/STOR* RH20 ....11 G2
Hampton Flds *LHPTN* BN17 ....34 A2
Ham Rd *WTHG* BN11........................40 D1
Ham Wy *WTHG* BN11.......................29 H5
Hangleton Gra *FERR* BN12................37 F1
Hangleton La *FERR* BN12..................26 A5
Hanover Wk *PUL/STOR* RH20...........10 D3
Harborough Cl *PUL/STOR* RH20 ....6 A1
Harborough Dr *PUL/STOR* RH20 ....6 A1
Harborough Gorse
   PUL/STOR RH20 ....6 A1
Harborough Meadow
   PUL/STOR RH20 ....6 A1
Hardbarrow Woods
   PUL/STOR RH20 ....7 F3
Hardham Cl *ANG/EP* BN16 ....35 E4
Harebell Cl *ANG/EP* BN16 ....35 E1
Harefield Av *SALV* BN13 ....28 A5
Harlech Cl *SALV* BN13 ....27 E4
Harrison Ct *FIN/BW* BN14.................29 F4
Harrison Rd *FIN/BW* BN14 ....29 F4
Harrow Rd *WTHG* BN11 ....2 A2
Harsfold Cl *ANG/EP* BN16 ....34 D4
Harsfold Rd *ANG/EP* BN16 ....35 E4
Harting Cl *FERR* BN12......................27 E5
Harting Rd *LHPTN* BN17 ....34 A1
Harvey Rd *FERR* BN12......................38 D3
Harwood Av *FERR* BN12...................27 G5
Harwood Rd *LHPTN* BN17 ....33 H2
Hastings Rd *WTHG* BN11 ....39 F3
The Haven *ANG/EP* BN16 ....34 D3
   LAN/SOMP * BN15......................31 E5
Hawke Cl *ANG/EP* BN16 ....35 H3
Hawley Rd *ANG/EP* BN16 ....35 E4
Hawthorn Crs *FIN/BW* BN14 ....29 E3
Hawthorn Gdns *FIN/BW* BN14.........29 E3
Hawthorn Rd *FIN/BW* BN14.............28 D3
   LHPTN BN17 ....23 E5
The Hawthorns *PUL/STOR* RH20......6 D2
Hawthorn Wy *PUL/STOR* RH20 ....10 C2
Hayley Rd *LAN/SOMP* BN15 ....31 E2
Hayling Gdns *SALV* BN13.................19 H5
Hayling Ri *SALV* BN13 ....19 H5
Haynes Rd *FIN/BW* BN14 ....28 B5
Haynes Wy *FIN/BW* BN14..................2 A1
Hazelhurst Crs *FIN/BW* BN14...........20 A3
Hazel Ldg *ANG/EP* * BN16 ....35 F4

Hazelmead Dr *ANG/EP* BN16...........36 B3
Hazelwood Cl *FIN/BW* BN14............29 G4
   PUL/STOR RH20 ....11 G2
Hearnfield Rd *LHPTN* BN17 ....23 E5
Heatherlands *PUL/STOR* RH20 ....11 E2
Heather La *PUL/STOR* RH20 ....6 A4
   SALV BN13 ....19 H4
The Heathers *ANG/EP* * BN16 ....25 E3
Heatherstone Rd *WTHG* BN11........40 D1
Heather Wy *PUL/STOR* RH20 ....11 E3
Heathfield Av *ANG/EP* BN16 ....36 A1
Heathfield Cl *SALV* BN13 ....28 A4
Heathfield Copse
   PUL/STOR RH20 ....6 A2
Heene Pl *WTHG* BN11 ....2 B6
Heene Rd *WTHG* BN11.......................2 B6
Heene Ter *WTHG* BN11 ....2 B7
Heene Wy *WTHG* BN11 ....2 A5
The Heights *FIN/BW* BN14 ....20 B5
Helyer's Gn *LHPTN* BN17 ....33 H2
Henderson Wk *STEY/UB* BN44 ....14 D1
Hendon Av *ANG/EP* BN16.................34 D5
Henfield Cl *FERR* BN12.....................27 E5
Henfield Rd *STEY/UB* BN44 ....15 C4
Henry Av *ANG/EP* BN16 ....34 D3
Henty Rd *FERR* BN12........................37 G4
   FIN/BW BN14..............................20 C1
Herington Rd *ARUN* BN18 ....21 E4
Hermione Ct *FERR* BN12 ....37 E1
Hermit Ter *FIN/BW* * BN14 ....13 H5
Herm Rd *FERR* BN12 ....20 C1
Herne Ct *ANG/EP* * BN16 ....35 G2
Herne Gdns *ANG/EP* BN16 ....35 G2
Herne La *ANG/EP* BN16....................35 G2
The Herons *LAN/SOMP* * BN15 ....31 E5
Hertford Rd *WTHG* BN11 ....2 E3
Hewitts *HFD* BN5 ....9 G4
Hewitts End *HFD* BN5.........................9 G4
Heyshott Cl *LAN/SOMP* BN15.........30 D1
Hide Gdns *ANG/EP* BN16..................35 E2
High Bar La *PUL/STOR* RH20 ....7 E3
Highbarn *FIN/BW* BN14 ....13 H4
Highbrook Pl *PUL/STOR* * RH20 ......10 C3
Highclere Wy *SALV* BN13 ....27 E4
Highdown Av *SALV* BN13 ....28 A1
Highdown Cl *FERR* BN12 ....37 F1
Highdown Dr *LHPTN* BN17 ....34 B2
Highdown Wy *FERR* BN12 ....37 F1
Highfield *LHPTN* BN17 ....33 G1
Highfield Cl *ANG/EP* BN16 ....25 E4
Highfield Gdns *ANG/EP* BN16 ....35 E4
Highfield Rd *SALV* BN13 ....28 B3
Highgrove Gdns *WTHG* BN11.............2 B5
Highlands Cl *SALV* BN13...................19 H5
High Ridge Cl *ARUN* BN18 ....21 E5
High Spinney *PUL/STOR* RH20...........6 D4
High St *ANG/EP* BN16.......................25 E4
   ARUN BN18 ....12 C1
   ARUN BN18 ....21 G3
   FIN/BW BN14..............................19 H1
   HFD BN5.......................................9 H4
   LHPTN BN17 ....34 A3
   PUL/STOR RH20 ....10 C3
   SALV BN13 ....28 B4
   STEY/UB BN44............................14 C2
   STEY/UB BN44............................15 F3
   WTHG BN11 ....3 J4
High Titten *ARUN* BN18 ....12 B3
High Vw *SALV* BN13 ....20 A5
Hildon Cl *SALV* BN13 ....27 G4
Hill Barn La *FIN/BW* BN14 ....28 D2
Hillbarn Pde *LAN/SOMP* * BN15....30 B1
Hillcrest Cl *PUL/STOR* RH20 ....8 C4
Hillcrest Dr *PUL/STOR* RH20.............8 C4
Hillcrest Pk *PUL/STOR* RH20..............5 E4
Hill Farm La *PUL/STOR* RH20 ....4 B1
Hillrise Av *LAN/SOMP* BN15 ....30 B1
Hill Rd *LHPTN* BN17 ....34 B2
Hillside Av *FIN/BW* BN14.................28 C2
Hillside Crs *ANG/EP* BN16 ....25 F4
Hillside Rd *LAN/SOMP* BN15............30 B1
   PUL/STOR RH20 ....10 C3
Hillside Wk *PUL/STOR* RH20 ....11 F2
Hills Rd *STEY/UB* BN44 ....14 D3
Hill Ter *ARUN* BN18 ....21 E4
Hillview Crs *ANG/EP* BN16 ....36 B2
Hillview Ri *FIN/BW* BN14..................20 A5
Hillview Rd *FIN/BW* BN14.................20 A4
Hindle Cl *PUL/STOR* RH20 ....6 C2
Hobart Cl *SALV* BN13 ....27 F2
Hobbs Cl *ANG/EP* BN16 ....35 F3
Hobs Acre *STEY/UB* BN44.................14 B5
Hog La *ARUN* BN18 ....12 C1
Hole St *PUL/STOR* RH20 ....8 C5
Holland Rd *STEY/UB* BN44 ....14 C2
Hollands La *HFD* BN5 ....9 E4
Hollands Rd *HFD* BN5.........................9 F3
Hollingbury Gdns *FIN/BW* BN14 .....20 B3

Hollyacres *SALV* BN13 ....27 F1
Holly Cl *PUL/STOR* RH20 ....10 B3
   SALV BN13 ....27 F4
Holly Ct *PUL/STOR* RH20 ....10 B2
Holly Dr *LHPTN* BN17 ....23 F5
Hollyhock Wy *ANG/EP* BN16 ....34 D1
Holmcroft Rd *WTHG* BN11 ....19 H1
Holmes Foundation
   ARUN * BN18 ....21 G4
Holmes La *ANG/EP* BN16 ....35 E4
Holmfield Cl *ANG/EP* BN16..............35 F2
Homefield Rd *WTHG* BN11 ....3 H2
Homelands Av *ANG/EP* BN16...........36 B4
Homewood *FIN/BW* BN14 ....13 H4
Honey La *ANG/EP* BN16 ....25 F4
Honeysuckle Cl *ANG/EP* BN16 ....34 D1
Honeysuckle La *SALV* BN13 ....19 F2
The Hooe *LHPTN* BN17 ....34 D3
The Hooks *HFD* BN5............................9 G4
Hormare Crs *PUL/STOR* RH20 ....10 B2
Horsemere Green La
   LHPTN BN17 ....32 B3
Horsham Rd *FIN/BW* BN14...............13 G3
   LHPTN BN17 ....25 F4
Horsham Rd West *LHPTN* BN17 ....34 C2
Houghton Br *ARUN* BN18.................12 B4
Howard Pl *LHPTN* BN17 ....34 A3
Howard Rd *ARUN* BN18 ....21 F4
   LHPTN BN17 ....33 H3
Howard St *WTHG* BN11......................2 E5
Howards Wy *ANG/EP* BN16 ....35 E5
Hudson Cl *SALV* BN13 ....27 G3
Hudson Dr *ANG/EP* BN16 ....35 G4
Humber Av *SALV* BN13 ....27 F2
Humber Cl *LHPTN* BN17 ....34 C4
   SALV BN13 ....27 F2
Humphrys Rd *WTHG* BN11 ....2 E5
Hurley Rd *SALV* BN13.......................27 H3
Hurst Av *WTHG* BN11 ....39 E2
Hurst Cl *ARUN* BN18 ....12 C1
Hurst Cottages *ARUN* BN18.............12 C1
Hurstfield *LAN/SOMP* BN15 ....30 C4
Hurston Cl *FIN/BW* BN14 ....28 B1
Hurston Gv *PUL/STOR* RH20............10 A2
Hurston La *PUL/STOR* RH20 ....10 A2
Hurst Rd *ANG/EP* BN16 ....35 H2
Hutchinson Cl *ANG/EP* BN16 ....35 E1
Hyde La *STEY/UB* BN44 ....15 G4
Hyde Sq *STEY/UB* * BN44 ....15 G4
Hyde St *STEY/UB* BN44 ....15 G3
Hythe Cl *WTHG* BN11 ....39 F3
Hythe Rd *WTHG* BN11 ....39 F3

I

Ilex Cl *ANG/EP* BN16 ....35 E4
Ilex Ct *FERR* * BN12 ....38 A2
Ilex Wy *FERR* BN12...........................38 A2
Inglecroft Ct *LAN/SOMP* * BN15 ....30 B2
Ingle Green Cl *FERR* BN12 ....37 F4
Ingleside Crs *LAN/SOMP* BN15........30 D4
Ingleside Rd *LAN/SOMP* BN15.........30 D4
Ingram Cl *ANG/EP* BN16 ....35 E3
Ingram Rd *STEY/UB* BN44 ....14 B3
Irene Av *LAN/SOMP* BN15................30 C2
Irvine Rd *LHPTN* BN17......................34 B4
Ivy Arch Rd *FIN/BW* BN14 ....3 F2
Ivy Cl *PUL/STOR* RH20........................8 C3
Ivydore Av *SALV* BN13 ....27 G1
Ivydore Cl *SALV* BN13 ....27 G2
Ivy La *PUL/STOR* RH20 ....8 C2
Ivy Pl *WTHG* BN11.............................2 B6

J

James Cl *SALV* BN13.........................28 A3
Jarvis La *STEY/UB* BN44 ....14 C2
Jarvis Rd *ARUN* BN18 ....21 E4
Jasmine Cl *ANG/EP* BN16 ....34 D1
Jays Cl *LHPTN* BN17 ....34 A2
Jefferies La *FERR* BN12....................38 B3
Jersey Rd *FERR* BN12.......................37 G3
Jervis Av *ANG/EP* BN16 ....35 E4
Jevington Cl *SALV* BN13 ....27 E4
Jib Cl *ANG/EP* BN16 ....34 D1
Johnson Wy *ARUN* BN18 ....32 A2
Joyce Cl *LHPTN* BN17 ....33 H1
Jubilee Av *ANG/EP* BN16 ....35 F2
Jubilee Wy *PUL/STOR* RH20 ....11 E1
Junction Cl *ARUN* BN18...................32 A2
Juniper Cl *SALV* BN13.......................27 F4
Juno Cl *FERR* BN12 ....38 B2
Jupp's La *FERR* BN12 ....38 A1

K

Kearsley Dr *FIN/BW* BN14................20
Keelson Wy *ANG/EP* BN16 34
Kelso Cl *SALV* BN13 27
Kendal Cl *LHPTN* BN17 34
Kendal Rd *LAN/SOMP* BN15 30
Kennet Cl *SALV* BN13.......................27
Kensington Cl *PUL/STOR* * RH20 6
Kent Rd *LHPTN* BN17 34
Kenwood Quay
   LAN/SOMP * BN15......................31
Kestrel Wy *LHPTN* BN17 22
Keswick Cl *FERR* BN12 27
Ketch Rd *LHPTN* BN17......................34
Keymer Crs *FERR* BN12....................27
Keymer Wy *FERR* BN12 38
Kilmore Cl *FIN/BW* BN14..................27
Kimber Cl *LAN/SOMP* BN15 30
Kinfauns Dr *SALV* BN13....................19
King Alfred Cl *STEY/UB* BN44 14
King Edward Av *FIN/BW* BN14............3
King Edward Cl *FIN/BW* BN14 3
Kingfisher Cl *SALV* BN13 27
Kingfisher Dr *LHPTN* BN17 22
King's Arms HI *ARUN* BN18 21
Kings Barn End *STEY/UB* * BN44......15
King's Barn Vls *STEY/UB* BN44 14
Kingsbridge Ms *SALV* BN13..............27
Kings Cl *LAN/SOMP* BN15 31
Kingsfield *PUL/STOR* RH20 6
Kingsland Cl *PUL/STOR* RH20...........10
Kingsland Rd *FIN/BW* BN14 29
Kings La *PUL/STOR* RH20 9
Kingsley Cl *FIN/BW* BN14 29
Kingsmead *LHPTN* BN17 22
Kingsmead Cl *STEY/UB* BN44 14
Kings Rd *LAN/SOMP* BN15 30
King's Stone Av *STEY/UB* BN44 15
Kingston La *ANG/EP* BN16 30
King St *ARUN* BN18 21
   FIN/BW BN14..............................20
Kingsway *FERR* * BN12.....................39
Kingswood *PUL/STOR* RH20 6
Kipling Av *FERR* BN12.......................38
Kirdford Cl *ANG/EP* BN16 34
Kirdford Rd *ARUN* BN18 21
Kirkland Cl *ANG/EP* BN16 35
Kithurst Cl *ANG/EP* BN16 35
   FERR BN12.................................27
Kithurst Crs *FERR* BN12 27
Kithurst Farm Rd
   PUL/STOR RH20 10
Kithurst La *PUL/STOR* RH20 10
Kithurst Pk *PUL/STOR* RH20.............10
Knightscroft Av *ANG/EP* BN16 35
Knightscroft Cl *ANG/EP* BN16 35

L

Laburnum Cl *FERR* BN12 37
   LAN/SOMP BN15........................30
Ladydell Rd *WTHG* BN11 2
Laines Rd *STEY/UB* BN44 14
Lambleys La *FIN/BW* BN14 29
Lammas Cl *LHPTN* BN17 34
Lamorna Gdns *FERR* BN12 37
Lamorna Gv *FERR* BN12....................28
Lancaster Rd *FERR* BN12 38
Lancing Cl *LAN/SOMP* BN15.............30
Lancing Pk *LAN/SOMP* BN15 30
Lanfranc Rd *FIN/BW* BN14.................2
Langbury Cl *FERR* BN12 37
Langbury La *FERR* BN12....................37
Langdale Cl *LAN/SOMP* BN15...........30
Langham Gdns *WTHG* BN11 32
Langmead Cl *LHPTN* BN17 32
Langmeads Cl *LHPTN* * BN17 32
Langton Pl *PUL/STOR* * RH20...........10
Langton Rd *FIN/BW* BN14 2
Lansdowne Cl *ANG/EP* BN16 25
Lansdowne Ct *WTHG* BN11 39
Lansdowne Pl *WTHG* BN11................2
Lansdowne Rd *ANG/EP* BN16 34
   LHPTN BN17 34
   WTHG BN11 39
Lansdowne Wy *ANG/EP* BN16...........25
Lanyards *LHPTN* BN17 34
Larch Cl *ANG/EP* BN16......................35
Larch End *PUL/STOR* RH20................10
Larkfield Cl *LAN/SOMP* BN15 31
Larkspur Cl *ANG/EP* BN16................34
Lashmar Rd *ANG/EP* BN16 35
Latimer Rd *WTHG* BN11 39

CI SALV BN13 ...27 F4
Mt PUL/STOR RH20 ...4 D4
urels HFD BN5 ...9 G3
CI FERR BN12 ...26 D5
ton Rd FIN/BW BN14 ...28 C3
Ct FERR BN12 ...38 B1
Wy ANG/EP BN16 ...36 B3
wns ANG/EP BN16 ...36 B5
SOMP BN15 ...30 B2
ice Av ANG/EP BN16 ...35 G2
's La HFD BN5 ...9 E3
's La ANG/EP BN16 ...35 H1
ield Rd LAN/SOMP BN15 ...30 B4
d SALV BN13 ...27 E4
rd CI SALV BN13 ...28 A4
d Rd LHPTN BN17 ...34 C3
BN13 ...28 A4
d FIN/BW BN14 ...29 E3
on Av FIN/BW BN14 ...29 F3
st Wy SALV BN13 ...28 A4
: Rd WTHG BN11 ...3 F3
orth Ct FERR BN12 ...37 F3
CI LAN/SOMP BN15 ...31 E2
t SALV BN13 ...27 E4
a ARUN BN18 ...32 A1
La LAN/SOMP BN15 ...30 C1
PI WTHG BN11 ...3 G5
nd Ct WTHG * BN11 ...39 F3
SALV BN13 ...27 E4
e FERR BN12 ...38 B1
ck FERR * BN12 ...27 F5
ck Cnr FERR * BN12 ...27 F5
ck FERR BN12 ...27 F5
ck Wy FERR BN12 ...27 E5
na PUL/STOR RH20 ...10 C2
d FIN/BW BN14 ...13 H4
es FIN/BW * BN14 ...13 H4
ee Av FIN/BW BN14 ...20 A5
ee CI ANG/EP * BN16 ...36 A4
n Av SALV BN13 ...28 A5
Dr SALV BN13 ...39 E1
s SALV BN13 ...28 A5
PI PUL/STOR * RH20 ...10 C3
Pk LHPTN BN17 ...33 H3
rd LHPTN BN17 ...33 H3
t Rd SALV BN13 ...28 A4
Wy SALV BN13 ...28 A4
e Wy LHPTN BN17 ...33 G2
Copse PUL/STOR RH20 ...7 E3
fields PUL/STOR * RH20 ...7 E3
d CI SALV BN13 ...28 A3
PUL/STOR RH20 ...10 A3
PUL/STOR RH20 ...4 D4
d FIN/BW BN14 ...28 B1
SOMP BN15 ...31 E3
kway WTHG * BN11 ...2 C3
td LAN/SOMP BN15 ...31 E2
pper's PUL/STOR RH20 ...4 D4
FERR BN12 ...37 F3
ro STEY/UB BN44 ...14 C4
ables SALV BN13 ...28 A3

mpton Marina
V * BN17 ...33 H3
mpton Rd
EP BN16 ...36 D1
BN12 ...27 E5
gh St WTHG BN11 ...3 F3
PUL/STOR RH20 ...6 B1
d FERR * BN12 ...38 B2
addocks Wy FERR BN12 ...37 G3
mbrokes WTHG BN11 ...39 F1
one Rd SALV BN13 ...27 H3
ol Gdns FIN/BW BN11 ...3 F5
ol Rd WTHG BN11 ...3 F5
ol Ter WTHG BN11 ...3 F5
Crs FIN/BW BN14 ...29 E5
eadow FIN/BW BN14 ...20 A2
oring CI ANG/EP BN16 ...25 E3
ood La PUL/STOR RH20 ...10 C2
r CI SALV BN13 ...27 F1
dns FIN/BW BN14 ...28 D4
d ARUN BN18 ...21 F3
BN5 ...9 G1
STOR RH20 ...4 C4
STOR RH20 ...8 C4
St WTHG BN11 ...2 C2
low Rd WTHG BN11 ...2 B3
rlong SALV BN13 ...18 B5
rlong La SALV BN13 ...18 B2
d Av PUL/STOR RH20 ...10 B2
ds FIN/BW BN14 ...28 D1
ds Gld FIN/BW BN14 ...29 E1
ds Spinney
BN14 ...29 E1
ps ANG/EP BN16 ...34 D2
s La FIN/BW BN14 ...29 H4
s La PUL/STOR RH20 ...6 C2
s LAN/SOMP BN15 ...30 B3

Loudoun Rd LHPTN BN17 ...33 H3
Lovett Ct FERR * BN12 ...27 F5
Lower Faircox HFD BN5 ...9 F3
Lower Station Rd HFD BN5 ...9 F4
Lower St PUL/STOR RH20 ...4 C4
Lowther Rd SALV BN13 ...28 A2
Loxley Gdns FIN/BW BN14 ...2 C1
Loxwood CI ANG/EP BN16 ...25 G1
Loxwood Av FIN/BW BN14 ...28 C1
Lundy CI ANG/EP BN16 ...34 D4
Lupin CI ANG/EP BN16 ...34 D1
Lyminster Rd LHPTN BN17 ...23 E4
Lynchmere Av LAN/SOMP BN15 ...30 C1
Lyndhurst Rd WTHG BN11 ...3 C4
Lyn Rd SALV BN13 ...27 F3
Lyntons PUL/STOR RH20 ...4 B4
Lyons Wy FIN/BW BN14 ...29 F1

M

Madehurst CI ANG/EP BN16 ...35 H4
Madehurst Wy LHPTN BN17 ...34 A2
Madeira Av WTHG BN11 ...3 H4
Magnolia CI SALV BN13 ...27 E4
Malcolm Ct FERR BN12 ...37 E2
Malden PI PUL/STOR * RH20 ...10 C3
Malin Rd ANG/EP BN16 ...34 D3
Mallard Wy HFD BN5 ...9 G2
Mallon Dene ANG/EP BN16 ...35 F4
Malthouse CI ARUN BN18 ...21 F4
  LAN/SOMP BN15 ...30 A2
Malthouse Pas LHPTN BN17 ...34 A2
Maltravers Dr LHPTN BN17 ...34 B4
Maltravers St ARUN BN18 ...21 E4
Malvern CI WTHG BN11 ...41 E1
Manitoba Wy SALV BN13 ...27 F3
Manley's HI PUL/STOR * RH20 ...10 C3
Manning Rd LHPTN BN17 ...33 H2
The Manor WTHG * BN11 ...2 B4
Manor CI ANG/EP BN16 ...36 A3
  HFD BN5 ...9 H3
  LAN/SOMP BN15 ...31 G3
  LAN/SOMP BN15 ...31 E2
  PUL/STOR RH20 ...10 C3
  WTHG BN11 ...2 A5
Manor Ct ANG/EP * BN16 ...35 E2
  LAN/SOMP * BN15 ...30 C1
  PUL/STOR * RH20 ...10 C3
Manor Field Ct FIN/BW * BN14 ...29 E4
Manor Lea WTHG * BN11 ...2 B6
Manor Pde SALV * BN13 ...27 G5
Manor Rd ANG/EP BN16 ...35 E2
  ANG/EP BN16 ...36 B4
  LAN/SOMP BN15 ...30 C1
  STEY/UB BN44 ...14 C3
  STEY/UB BN44 ...15 H3
  WTHG BN11 ...2 A5
Manor View Ct FIN/BW * BN14 ...29 E4
Manor Wy HFD BN5 ...9 H2
  LAN/SOMP BN15 ...31 E2
Mansfield CI WTHG BN11 ...29 H5
Mansfield Rd WTHG BN11 ...40 D1
Mant CI LHPTN BN17 ...32 C3
  PUL/STOR RH20 ...10 C3
Mantling Rd LHPTN BN17 ...34 A2
The Maples FERR BN12 ...37 E2
Maple CI SALV BN13 ...19 H5
Maple Wk LAN/SOMP BN15 ...30 A2
Marama Gdns ANG/EP BN16 ...35 E5
Mardale Rd SALV BN13 ...28 A3
Mare Hill Rd PUL/STOR RH20 ...5 F4
Marigolds Ldg ANG/EP * BN16 ...35 E4
Marine Crs FIN/BW BN14 ...29 E5
Marine Dr FERR BN12 ...37 H4
Marine Pde FERR BN12 ...2 C7
Marine PI WTHG BN11 ...3 G6
The Mariners LAN/SOMP * BN15 ...41 G1
Mariners Wk ANG/EP BN16 ...35 G5
Market Fld STEY/UB BN44 ...14 C2
Market St WTHG BN11 ...3 G5
Markwick Ms WTHG BN11 ...3 G3
Marlborough Rd FERR BN12 ...38 B2
  LAN/SOMP BN15 ...30 B5
Marlborough Wy FERR * BN12 ...38 B2
Marley Wy PUL/STOR RH20 ...10 D2
Marlowe Rd FIN/BW BN14 ...29 E5
Marshall Av FIN/BW BN14 ...20 A3
Marston Rd FIN/BW BN14 ...29 F5
The Martlets ANG/EP BN16 ...34 D5
Martlets PUL/STOR RH20 ...6 B2
  LAN/SOMP BN15 ...30 B3
Martlets Wy FERR BN12 ...38 B1
Martyn CI HFD BN5 ...9 G3
Masons Wy PUL/STOR RH20 ...4 D1

Maudlin La STEY/UB BN44 ...14 C4
Maudlin CI STEY/UB BN44 ...14 D4
Maudlyn Pk STEY/UB BN44 ...14 C4
Maudlyn Pkwy STEY/UB BN44 ...14 C4
Maxwell Rd ARUN BN18 ...21 E5
  LHPTN BN17 ...33 H3
Maybridge Crs FERR BN12 ...38 B1
Maybridge Sq FERR BN12 ...27 F5
May CI FERR BN12 ...27 F5
Mayfield ANG/EP BN16 ...36 B1
Mayfield CI FIN/BW BN14 ...20 B5
Mayflower Wy ANG/EP BN16 ...36 B1
May Tree Av FIN/BW BN14 ...20 A3
Maytree CI ANG/EP BN16 ...25 E5
  LAN/SOMP BN15 ...30 A3
Mckerchar CI LAN/SOMP BN15 ...31 E2
Mead La PUL/STOR RH20 ...10 D2
Meadowbank PUL/STOR * RH20 ...5 E1
Meadow CI WTHG BN11 ...41 E1
Meadow Crs WTHG BN11 ...40 D1
Meadow La LAN/SOMP BN15 ...30 D1
Meadow Pk ANG/EP BN16 ...36 C3
Meadow Rd WTHG BN11 ...40 D1
Meadowside ANG/EP BN16 ...25 F3
  PUL/STOR RH20 ...10 C3
Meadowside Ct FERR * BN12 ...37 H2
Meadow Sweet CI SALV * BN13 ...26 D4
Meadowview Rd
  LAN/SOMP BN15 ...30 C1
Meadow Wy FERR BN12 ...37 F2
  LHPTN BN17 ...34 C3
Meadway ANG/EP BN16 ...35 G3
Meadway Ct SALV * BN13 ...27 H5
Measham CI FERR BN12 ...37 G3
Medway CI SALV BN13 ...27 G2
Meiros Wy PUL/STOR RH20 ...8 B1
Melbourne Av SALV BN13 ...38 B2
Melbourne Rd FERR BN12 ...38 B2
Melrose Av SALV BN13 ...27 H5
Melrose CI SALV BN13 ...27 H5
Melrose PI PUL/STOR RH20 ...11 H1
Melton Av ANG/EP BN16 ...10 C1
Melton CI PUL/STOR RH20 ...10 D1
Melton Dr PUL/STOR RH20 ...10 C1
Melville Wy FERR BN12 ...27 F5
Mendip CI ANG/EP BN16 ...36 B2
Mendip Crs SALV BN13 ...27 H2
Mendip Rd SALV BN13 ...27 H2
Meredith Rd FIN/BW BN14 ...3 J1
Merrifield Crs ANG/EP BN16 ...25 F3
Merryfield Rd PUL/STOR RH20 ...10 C2
Merryfield Wy PUL/STOR RH20 ...10 C2
Merrywood La PUL/STOR RH20 ...7 F5
Mersey CI SALV BN13 ...27 F2
Mersey Rd SALV BN13 ...27 F2
Mersham Gdns FERR BN12 ...38 B2
Merton Av ANG/EP BN16 ...35 F4
Merton Dr LHPTN BN17 ...34 A2
Merton Rd WTHG BN11 ...3 J5
The Mews ARUN BN18 ...21 C4
  PUL/STOR * RH20 ...4 D4
  PUL/STOR * RH20 ...2 C4
  WTHG * BN11 ...2 C4
Michel Gv ANG/EP BN16 ...35 H3
Middle Md STEY/UB BN44 ...14 C1
Middle Onslow CI FERR * BN12 ...37 F1
Middle Rd LAN/SOMP BN15 ...30 C4
Middle Tyne SALV BN13 ...27 G4
Middle Wy ANG/EP BN16 ...27 H2
Midhurst CI FERR BN12 ...37 G2
Midhurst Dr FERR BN12 ...37 G2
Milbury Rd FERR BN12 ...37 G4
Miles CI ARUN BN18 ...32 A2
Mill CI ANG/EP BN16 ...35 G2
Mill Ct WTHG * BN11 ...2 B4
Mill Dr HFD BN5 ...9 H4
Mill End HFD BN5 ...9 H4
  PUL/STOR RH20 ...6 B2
Millennium CI LAN/SOMP BN15 ...31 G3
Millers CI ANG/EP BN16 ...35 G2
Millfield LAN/SOMP BN15 ...30 B2
  STEY/UB * BN44 ...15 F3
Millfield CI ANG/EP BN16 ...35 E5
Mill House Gdns WTHG BN11 ...39 F2
Mill La ANG/EP BN16 ...35 G2
  ARUN BN18 ...12 C2
  ARUN BN18 ...21 G3
  LHPTN BN17 ...23 E4
  PUL/STOR RH20 ...6 B1
  PUL/STOR RH20 ...8 B2
  PUL/STOR RH20 ...10 C2
  SALV BN13 ...20 A4
Mill Md PUL/STOR RH20 ...8 C4
Mill Pond Wy ANG/EP BN16 ...36 A2
Mill Rd ANG/EP BN16 ...25 E4
  ARUN BN18 ...21 G3
  LAN/SOMP BN15 ...30 D1
  PUL/STOR RH20 ...8 B1

STEY/UB BN44 ...14 B2
WTHG BN11 ...2 B4
Mill Road Av ANG/EP BN16 ...25 E5
Milton Av ANG/EP BN16 ...35 E4
Milton CI ANG/EP BN16 ...35 E3
  LAN/SOMP BN15 ...30 D4
Milton Rd WTHG BN11 ...2 C6
Milton St WTHG BN11 ...2 C6
Mimmack CI STEY/UB BN44 ...14 C1
Minster Ct LHPTN * BN17 ...22 D5
The Moat PUL/STOR RH20 ...4 D4
Moat CI PUL/STOR RH20 ...4 D4
Moat Wy FERR BN12 ...38 D3
The Mole LHPTN BN17 ...34 D3
Monarch's Wy SALV BN13 ...13 E5
  STEY/UB BN44 ...14 D4
Monastery La PUL/STOR RH20 ...10 B3
Monkmead Copse
  PUL/STOR RH20 ...6 B3
Monkmead La PUL/STOR RH20 ...6 A2
Monks Av LAN/SOMP BN15 ...31 E3
Monks CI LAN/SOMP BN15 ...30 D3
Monks Wk STEY/UB BN44 ...15 G3
Montague PI WTHG BN11 ...3 F6
Montague St WTHG BN11 ...2 E6
Montgomeri Dr ANG/EP BN16 ...35 E1
Montpelier Rd ANG/EP BN16 ...36 B3
Montreal Wy SALV BN13 ...27 F3
Montrose CI FERR BN12 ...38 B1
Moore CI SALV BN13 ...27 E3
Moorfoot Rd SALV BN13 ...28 A2
The Moorings LAN/SOMP BN15 ...31 E1
Morland Av FIN/BW BN14 ...29 F2
Morleys PUL/STOR RH20 ...8 C4
Morris Wy PUL/STOR RH20 ...6 B2
Mountbatten Ct ANG/EP * BN16 ...34 D2
Mount Pleasant ARUN BN18 ...21 F3
Mountview Rd LAN/SOMP BN15 ...30 B1
Mouse La STEY/UB BN44 ...14 A1
Muirfield CI SALV BN13 ...27 H3
Muirfield Rd SALV BN13 ...27 G3
Mulberry CI FERR BN12 ...37 F2
  FERR BN12 ...38 B1
  LAN/SOMP BN15 ...30 D3
Mulberry Ct FERR BN12 ...38 B2
Mulberry Gdns FERR BN12 ...38 B2
Mulberry La FERR BN12 ...38 B2
Mulberry Ldg ANG/EP * BN16 ...35 F5
Munmere Wy ANG/EP * BN16 ...35 H2
Mustang CI ARUN BN18 ...32 A1
Myrtle Crs LAN/SOMP BN15 ...30 B4
Myrtle Gv ANG/EP BN16 ...35 H3
Myrtle Rd LAN/SOMP BN15 ...30 C4
Myrtle Ter HFD * BN5 ...9 G4

N

Navarino Rd WTHG BN11 ...40 D1
Nelson CI LAN/SOMP BN15 ...30 C1
Nelson Rd FERR BN12 ...27 C5
Nelson Rw ARUN BN18 ...32 D1
Nepcote La FIN/BW BN14 ...13 H5
Nepfield CI FIN/BW BN14 ...19 H1
Nep Town Rd HFD BN5 ...9 G4
Neptune Wy ANG/EP BN16 ...34 D4
New Barn La PUL/STOR RH20 ...6 A1
New Barn Rd ARUN BN18 ...12 B3
New Broadway FIN/BW * BN14 ...39 F1
New Courtwick La LHPTN BN17 ...22 D5
New Cut ARUN BN18 ...21 G3
New Gdns FIN/BW * BN14 ...29 C2
Newham CI STEY/UB BN44 ...14 B2
Newham La STEY/UB BN44 ...14 A3
Newhouse La PUL/STOR RH20 ...11 H1
Newland Rd STEY/UB BN44 ...15 C3
  WTHG BN11 ...3 F2
Newland St WTHG BN11 ...3 F2
Newling Wy SALV BN13 ...19 H5
Newman's Gdns
  LAN/SOMP BN15 ...30 A2
New Pde WTHG BN11 ...3 J5
New Place Rd PUL/STOR RH20 ...4 D3
Newport Ms WTHG BN11 ...41 E1
New Rd ANG/EP BN16 ...35 C1
  LHPTN BN17 ...34 A4
  SALV BN13 ...27 F2
  STEY/UB BN44 ...15 C4
New Salts Farm Rd SHOR BN43 ...31 H3
New St WTHG BN11 ...2 E6
Newtimber Av FERR BN12 ...38 A1
New Town Rd PUL/STOR RH20 ...10 A3
Nightingale CI PUL/STOR RH20 ...10 D3
Nightingale La PUL/STOR RH20 ...10 D3
Nightingale Pk PUL/STOR RH20 ...10 D3
Nightingales FIN/BW BN14 ...13 H4
  PUL/STOR RH20 ...6 C2

Nimbus Cl LHPTN BN17 .....34 D2
The Nookery ANG/EP BN16 .....36 B3
Norbury Cl LAN/SOMP BN15 .....31 E1
Norbury Dr LAN/SOMP BN15 .....30 D1
Norfolk Ct WTHG * BN11.....2 C3
Norfolk Gdns LHPTN BN17 .....34 C4
Norfolk Ms LHPTN * BN17 .....34 C4
Norfolk Pl LHPTN BN17 .....34 C4
Norfolk Rd LHPTN BN17 .....34 C4
Norfolk St WTHG BN11 .....2 C3
Norman Cl LHPTN BN17 .....34 C4
Normandy Dr ANG/EP BN16 .....36 A4
Normandy La ANG/EP BN16 .....36 B4
Normandy Rd FIN/BW BN14 .....28 D5
Normanhurst Cl ANG/EP BN16 .....35 F4
Norman Wy STEY/UB BN44 .....14 C1
North Av FERR BN12 .....38 D3
Northbrook Cl FIN/BW BN14 .....29 F3
Northbrook Rd FIN/BW BN14 .....29 F3
Northcourt Cl ANG/EP BN16 .....35 G2
Northcourt Rd FIN/BW BN14 .....2 D1
Northcroft HFD BN5
North Dr ANG/EP BN16 .....25 E5
North Farm Rd
  LAN/SOMP BN15 .....30 D3
Northfield Rd LAN/SOMP BN13 .....28 B3
Northgate Cl LAN/SOMP BN15 .....30 A3
North Ham Rd LHPTN BN17 .....34 A3
Northlands La PUL/STOR RH20 .....6 D5
North La ANG/EP BN16 .....35 E2
  ANG/EP BN16 .....36 B3
North Pl LHPTN BN17 .....34 B4
North Rd LAN/SOMP BN15 .....30 D3
North St LHPTN BN17 .....34 A1
  PUL/STOR RH20 .....10 C3
  WTHG BN11 .....3 F3
Northview Ter FIN/BW * BN14 .....13 H5
Northway Rd LHPTN BN17 .....23 E5
Norton Rd LAN/SOMP BN15 .....30 C4
Norway La LHPTN BN17 .....34 C1
Norwich Ct WTHG * BN11 .....39 F3
Nursery Cl ANG/EP BN16 .....36 B4
  LAN/SOMP BN15 .....30 C1
Nursery Gdns LHPTN BN17 .....34 A1
Nursery La WTHG BN11 .....2 C6
Nutbourne La PUL/STOR RH20 .....5 H2
Nutbourne Rd FIN/BW BN14 .....28 C5
  PUL/STOR RH20 .....5 H5
Nutcroft PUL/STOR RH20 .....4 D3
Nutley Av FERR BN12 .....38 B3
Nutley Cl FERR BN12 .....38 B3
Nutley Crs FERR BN12 .....38 B3
Nutley Dr FERR BN12 .....38 B5
Nyes Cl HFD BN5 .....9 H3
Nytimber Cl PUL/STOR RH20 .....6 B3
Nyetimber Copse
  PUL/STOR RH20 .....6 B2
Nyetimber La PUL/STOR RH20 .....6 A2

O

Oak Av PUL/STOR RH20 .....11 G1
Oak Cl PUL/STOR RH20 .....11 E2
  SALV BN13 .....19 H5
Oakcroft Gdns LHPTN BN17 .....34 C1
Oak End PUL/STOR RH20 .....6 C2
Oakhurst HFD BN5 .....9 G2
Oakhurst Gdns ANG/EP BN16 .....35 H2
Oakleigh Cl WTHG BN11 .....29 H5
Oakleigh Rd FIN/BW BN14 .....29 H5
Oakley Gdns ANG/EP BN16 .....36 B4
The Oaks ANG/EP BN16 .....35 H3
Oakvale PUL/STOR * RH20 .....6 B2
Ocean Cl FERR BN12 .....37 F4
Ocean Dr FERR BN12 .....37 F4
Ocean Pde FERR * BN12 .....37 F3
Offington Av FIN/BW BN14 .....28 C2
Offington Ct FIN/BW BN14 .....28 D3
Offington Dr FIN/BW BN14 .....28 C2
Offington Gdns FIN/BW BN14 .....28 D3
Offington La FIN/BW BN14 .....28 B3
Old Br PUL/STOR RH20 .....4 C5
Older Wy ANG/EP BN16 .....25 E3
Old Manor Rd ANG/EP BN16 .....35 E2
Old Market Sq STEY/UB * BN44 .....14 D2
Old Mead Rd LHPTN BN17 .....22 D1
The Old Ml ARUN * BN18 .....21 G3
Old Mill Dr PUL/STOR RH20 .....10 C3
Old Mill Pl PUL/STOR RH20 .....5 E5
Old Printing House Sq
  ARUN * BN18 .....21 G3
Old Salts Farm Rd
  LAN/SOMP BN15 .....31 E4
Old Shoreham Rd
  LAN/SOMP BN15 .....31 E1
Old Stocks FIN/BW * BN14 .....13 H5

Old Worthing Rd ANG/EP BN16.....36 C2
Onslow Dr FERR BN12.....37 F2
Ontario Cl SALV BN13 .....27 F3
Ontario Gdns SALV BN13.....27 F3
Ophir Rd WTHG BN11 .....40 D1
Orchard Av FIN/BW BN14.....28 B4
  LAN/SOMP BN15.....30 D2
Orchard Cl FERR BN12 .....37 F1
  FIN/BW BN14.....28 C4
Orchard Gdns ANG/EP BN16 .....35 G2
Orchard Pl ARUN BN18.....21 G3
Orchard Rd FERR BN12.....36 B2
Orchard Wy LAN/SOMP BN15 .....30 D2
  PUL/STOR RH20.....4 D3
Orient Rd LAN/SOMP BN15 .....31 H4
Orkney Ct SALV BN13.....27 E4
Orme Rd WTHG BN11.....2 C2
Osborne Cl LAN/SOMP BN15 .....30 B3
Osborne Dr LAN/SOMP BN15.....30 B3
Osmonde Cl FIN/BW BN14.....2 D1
The Oval FIN/BW BN14 .....13 H4
  SALV BN13.....28 A4
Oval Waye FERR BN12.....37 F4
Overstrand Av ANG/EP BN16.....35 E5
Oxford Rd WTHG BN11.....2 D3
Oxford Ter STEY/UB * BN44.....14 C2

P

The Paddock LHPTN BN17 .....22 D3
Paddock Cl FIN/BW * BN14.....28 C5
Paddock Gn ANG/EP BN16.....35 H2
The Paddocks LAN/SOMP BN15 .....31 E4
  STEY/UB BN44.....15 G2
Paddock Wy FIN/BW BN14 .....13 H5
Pages La WTHG BN11.....40 D1
Palatine Rd FERR BN12.....27 F5
The Pallant FERR BN12.....27 F5
Palma Ct WTHG * BN11.....2 A5
Palm Ct SALV BN13.....27 H2
Palmer Cl PUL/STOR RH20 .....11 E2
Palmer Rd LHPTN BN16.....24 D3
Palmerston Av FERR BN12.....38 B2
Palmers Wy SALV BN13.....19 G5
The Pantiles FERR * BN12 .....37 F3
The Parade ANG/EP * BN16 .....36 B4
Parade Man ANG/EP * BN16.....36 B4
Parham Cl ANG/EP BN16.....35 E4
  FIN/BW BN14.....20 A5
  LHPTN BN17.....34 A2
Parham Rd FIN/BW BN14.....20 A5
Park Av WTHG BN11.....3 H2
Park Cl FIN/BW BN14.....28 B2
Park Crs WTHG BN11.....2 D4
Park Dr ANG/EP BN16.....35 G2
  FERR BN12.....37 G2
Parkfield Ct SALV BN13.....28 B5
Parkfield Rd SALV BN13.....28 B5
Parklands Av FERR BN12.....38 C3
Park Pl ARUN BN18.....21 F3
Park Rd HFD BN5.....9 G4
  WTHG BN11.....3 G2
Parkside WTHG * BN11.....3 G3
Parkside La LHPTN BN17.....34 C3
Park View Ct ANG/EP * BN16.....35 F2
The Parkway ANG/EP BN16.....35 G3
Parry Dr ANG/EP BN16.....35 E3
Parsonage Rd HFD BN5.....9 G3
Parson's Hl ARUN BN18.....21 G3
Patching Cl FERR BN12.....27 E5
Paterson Wilson Rd
  LHPTN BN17.....34 B3
Patricia Av FERR BN12.....38 C3
Patricia Cl FERR BN12.....38 C3
Pavilion Pde WTHG * BN11.....3 F6
Pavilion Rd FIN/BW BN14.....2 B2
Paxmead Crs FIN/BW BN14.....29 C3
Peak La ANG/EP BN16.....36 D4
Pearson Rd ARUN BN18.....21 E4
Pearsons Retreat WTHG * BN11 .....41 F1
Pebble Wk ANG/EP BN16.....34 D1
Peel Cl LHPTN BN17.....33 H2
Pelham Rd SALV BN13.....28 A4
Pemberton Cl LAN/SOMP BN15.....30 D2
Pembroke Av WTHG BN11.....39 E2
Pembury Cl FIN/BW BN14.....2 E1
Penarth Gdns LHPTN BN17.....22 D4
Pende Cl LAN/SOMP BN15.....30 C1
Pendine Av WTHG BN11.....40 D1
Penfold La ANG/EP BN16.....35 F1
Penfold Rd FIN/BW BN14.....29 F3
Penfolds Pl ARUN BN18.....21 F4
Penfold Wy STEY/UB BN44.....14 C3
Penhill Rd LAN/SOMP BN15.....31 E4
Penland's Cl STEY/UB BN44.....14 C3
Penlands Ri STEY/UB BN44.....14 B3

Penlands V STEY/UB BN44.....14 B3
Penlands Wy STEY/UB BN44 .....14 C3
Penleigh Cl LAN/SOMP BN15 .....31 E4
Penns Ct STEY/UB BN44.....14 B1
Pennycress Av FERR BN12.....26 D4
Penstone Pk LAN/SOMP BN15.....30 C3
Pentland Rd SALV BN13 .....27 H2
Pepperscoombe La
  STEY/UB BN44.....15 F2
Peregrine Rd LHPTN BN17.....34 C3
Perrots La STEY/UB BN44.....14 B3
Peter Rd LAN/SOMP BN15.....30 B5
Petworth Av FERR BN12.....38 B4
Pevensey Gdn WTHG BN11.....39 F3
Pevensey Rd WTHG BN11.....39 E3
Peverel Rd SALV BN13.....28 B5
Peveril Cl SALV BN13.....29 H3
Peveril Dr LAN/SOMP BN15.....29 H3
Phrosso Rd WTHG BN11.....39 E3
Pier Rd LHPTN BN17.....34 A4
Pigeonhouse La ANG/EP BN16.....35 H4
Pilgrims Ter SALV * BN13.....39 F1
Pilgrims Wk SALV BN13.....39 F1
Pine Cl PUL/STOR RH20.....11 H4
Pines Av FIN/BW BN14.....29 E2
The Pines ANG/EP BN16.....25 E5
Pine Trees Cl ANG/EP BN16.....25 E2
Pinewood Cl ANG/EP BN16.....36 B2
The Plantation ANG/EP BN16.....36 B3
  PUL/STOR RH20.....10 A3
  SALV BN13.....28 A2
Plantation Cl SALV BN13.....28 A2
Plantation Ri SALV BN13.....28 B2
Plantation Wy PUL/STOR RH20.....10 B3
  SALV BN13.....28 A2
Plaza Pde WTHG * BN11.....2 D6
Poling Cl FERR BN12.....27 E5
Poling St ARUN BN18.....23 H3
Polperro Cl FERR BN12.....37 E3
Pond La SALV BN13.....27 G2
Pond Ms SALV * BN13.....27 G3
Poplar Rd SALV BN13.....27 F4
Poppy Cl ANG/EP BN16.....34 D1
Portland Av ANG/EP BN16.....34 D2
Portland Rd WTHG BN11.....2 E1
Portland Sq WTHG * BN11.....2 E5
Portway STEY/UB BN44.....14 B3
Posthorses PUL/STOR RH20.....8 C1
Post Vw PUL/STOR RH20.....10 D4
Potters Md LHPTN BN17.....33 H1
Poulter's La FIN/BW BN14.....28 C1
Pound La STEY/UB BN44.....15 C3
Pratton Av LAN/SOMP BN15.....30 C2
Preston Av ANG/EP BN16.....35 G3
Preston Hall Ms ANG/EP * BN16 .....36 A2
Preston Paddock ANG/EP BN16 .....35 H3
Prince Av LAN/SOMP BN15.....31 G4
Princess Av SALV BN13.....39 E1
Prince William Cl FIN/BW BN14.....28 B1
Priory Cl LAN/SOMP BN15.....30 A2
  SALV BN13.....28 B5
Priory Fld STEY/UB BN44.....15 F3
Priory Rd ANG/EP BN16.....35 E2
  ARUN BN18.....21 E5
Prospect Pl WTHG BN11.....2 E6
Providence Ter WTHG BN11.....3 G4
Pulborough Rd PUL/STOR RH20 .....10 A2
Purbeck Pl LHPTN BN17.....33 H3

Q

The Quadrangle FIN/BW BN14 .....19 H1
The Quadrant FERR BN12.....38 B1
Quantock Cl SALV BN13.....28 A1
Quantock Rd SALV BN13.....28 A1
The Quantocks LHPTN * BN17.....34 A2
The Quashetts FIN/BW BN14.....3 F1
Quayside LHPTN BN17.....33 C3
Queens La ARUN BN18.....21 G4
Queens Pde LAN/SOMP * BN15.....30 D3
Queens Rd LAN/SOMP BN15.....31 E5
  WTHG BN11.....2 C6
Queen St ARUN BN18.....21 G3
  FIN/BW BN14.....28 D5
  LHPTN BN17.....34 A3
Queensway LAN/SOMP BN15.....30 D3

R

Rackham Cl SALV BN13.....28 A4
Rackham Rd ANG/EP * BN16.....35 E5
  ARUN BN18.....12 D1
  SALV BN13.....28 A4
Rackham St ARUN BN18.....12 D1

Radnor Cl SALV * BN13
Radnor Rd SALV BN13
Raglan Av SALV BN13
Railway Ap WTHG BN11
Rainbow Wy PUL/STOR RH20
Raleigh Crs FERR BN12
Raleigh Wy FERR BN12
Rambledown La PUL/STOR RH20
Rapley Av PUL/STOR RH20
Rathbone Ct PUL/STOR * RH20
Ravenscroft ANG/EP * BN16
  PUL/STOR RH20
Rawson Vis ANG/EP * BN16
Rayden Cl LHPTN BN17
Rectory Cl PUL/STOR RH20
  PUL/STOR RH20
  PUL/STOR RH20
Rectory Farm Rd
  LAN/SOMP BN15
Rectory Gdns FIN/BW BN14
Rectory La ANG/EP BN16
  PUL/STOR RH20
Rectory Rd FIN/BW BN14
  PUL/STOR RH20
Rectory Wk LAN/SOMP BN15
  PUL/STOR RH20
Redwing Cl LHPTN BN17
Redwood Cl SALV BN13
Reed Cl PUL/STOR RH20
Reef Cl LHPTN BN17
Regent Cl LAN/SOMP BN15
Reigate Rd WTHG BN11
Renn Gdns PUL/STOR RH20
Richmond Ct ANG/EP BN16
Richmond Ct WTHG BN11
Richmond Rd WTHG BN11
The Ridings ANG/EP BN16
  STEY/UB BN44
Rifeside Gdns FERR BN12
Rife Wy FERR BN12
Ringmer Rd SALV BN13
Ripley Rd WTHG BN11
Ripon Ct WTHG * BN11
Rivermead PUL/STOR RH20
River Rd ARUN BN18
  LHPTN BN17
Riverside PUL/STOR RH20
  STEY/UB BN44
Robell Wy PUL/STOR RH20
Roberts Rd LAN/SOMP BN15
Robin Cl LHPTN BN17
Robinson Cl LAN/SOMP BN15
Robson Ct WTHG * BN11
Robson Rd WTHG BN11
Rochester Ct SALV BN13
Rochester Ct WTHG * BN11
Rockall Cl ANG/EP BN16
Rockingham Cl SALV BN13
Rockingham Ct SALV * BN13
Rock Rd PUL/STOR RH20
Rodmell Rd SALV BN13
Rodney Crs ARUN BN18
Roedean Rd SALV BN13
Rogate Cl LAN/SOMP BN15
  SALV BN13
Rogate Rd SALV BN13
Roger's La FIN/BW BN14
Rollaston Pk ARUN BN18
Roman Acre LHPTN BN17
Roman Rd STEY/UB BN44
Roman Wk LAN/SOMP BN15
Romany Rd SALV BN13
Romney Rd WTHG BN11
Rope Wk LHPTN BN17
Rosebery Av FERR BN12
Rosecroft Cl LAN/SOMP BN15
Rosemary Av STEY/UB BN44
Rosemary Cl PUL/STOR RH20
  STEY/UB BN44
Rosemead LHPTN BN17
Rose Pl ANG/EP BN16
Rose Wk FERR BN12
Rossiter Rd LAN/SOMP BN15
Rother Cl PUL/STOR RH20
Rothesay Cl SALV BN13
Roundabout Copse
  PUL/STOR RH20
Roundabout La
  PUL/STOR RH20
Roundstone By-Pass Rd
  ANG/EP BN16
Roundstone Crs ANG/EP BN16
Roundstone Dr ANG/EP BN16
Roundstone La ANG/EP BN16
The Roundway ANG/EP BN16
The Rowans WTHG BN11
Rowlands Rd WTHG BN11
Roxburgh Cl SALV BN13

oyal Ar *WTHG* BN11 ....3 F6
' Buildings
I/SOMP * BN15 ....30 C5
oystons *ANG/EP* BN16 ....36 A4
wick Av *FERR* BN12 ....37 H2
wick Cl *ANG/EP* BN16 ....35 E4
n Rd *FIN/BW* BN14 ....39 F1
n Rd *SALV* BN13 ....29 G5
er Rd *SALV* BN13 ....28 A4
er Rd South *SALV* BN13 .....28 A4
ell Cl *FIN/BW* BN14 ....29 F4
ell's Cl *ANG/EP* BN16 ....36 C2
ells Dr *LAN/SOMP* BN15 ....30 D4
on Av *ANG/EP* BN16 ....35 G3
on Pk *ANG/EP* BN16 ....35 H3
oft Cl *FERR* BN12 ....38 B3
oft Cl *ANG/EP* * BN16 ....34 D2
'l *WTHG* BN11 ....39 F3
oft Gdns *FERR* BN12 ....38 B3
oft La *PUL/STOR* RH20 .....10 C3

S

ville Crs *FIN/BW* BN14 ....29 F5
ville Rd *FIN/BW* BN14 ....3 G1
ville Wy *FIN/BW* BN14 ....3 H1
drew's Cl *FERR* BN12 ....37 F2
drews Gdns *SALV* BN13 .....28 B5
drew's Rd *SALV* BN13 ....28 A5
selm's Rd *FIN/BW* BN14 .....2 A1
thony's Wy *ANG/EP* BN16...35 G2
bins Rd *FERR* BN12 ....37 G4
ugustine Rd *LHPTN* BN17 ...34 B4
rnards Ct *LAN/SOMP* BN15 .30 D4
tolph's Rd *WTHG* BN11 ....2 A2
therine's Rd *LHPTN* BN17 ...34 A4
nstan's Rd *SALV* BN13 ....39 F1
no Rd *FIN/BW* BN14 ....2 B1
ra's La *LHPTN* BN17 ....34 C3
ra's Wy *LHPTN* BN17 ....34 C3
lier Rd *FERR* BN12 ....37 F2
nes Av *LAN/SOMP* BN15 .....30 D1
nn's Dr *ANG/EP* BN16 ....34 A3
nn's Cl *FERR* BN12 ....38 B3
nn's Rd *FERR* BN12 ....38 B3
wrence Av *FIN/BW* BN14 ....28 C5
es Cl *WTHG* BN11 ....30 A5
lo Cl *FERR* BN12 ....37 G4
ark's Crs *WTHG* BN11 ....34 A5
rtin's La *LHPTN* * BN17 ....34 A3
rtins Rd *LHPTN* * BN17 ....34 A3
rys Cl *LAN/SOMP* BN15 ......29 H2
TN BN17 ....34 B3
I/STOR RH20 ....4 D4
ry's Dr *ANG/EP* BN16 ....36 A3
ry's Gdns *LHPTN* * BN17 ....34 B3
ry's Gate Ms *ARUN* * BN18...21 F3
ry's Wy * BN17.............34 B3
ur's Rd *FERR* BN12 ....37 F2
chael's Ct *WTHG* BN11 ....2 A4
HG BN11 ....39 F2
chael's Rd *WTHG* BN11......2 A5
mund Rd *FERR* BN12 ....37 E2
ul's Av *WTHG* BN11 ....30 A5
ters Pl *LAN/SOMP* * BN15 ...30 B5
phael's La *LHPTN* * BN17 ...39 E2
omas's Rd *FIN/BW* BN14 ....28 C5
erie Rd *WTHG* BN11 ....39 F3
fred's Rd *LHPTN* BN17 ....34 B4
nefride's Rd *LHPTN* BN17 ...34 B4
bury Rd *WTHG* BN11 ....2 B5
altings *ANG/EP* BN16 ....34 D2
OMP * BN15 ....31 E4
gs Wy *STEY/UB* BN44 ....15 E3
agton Cl *SALV* BN13 ....27 H2
agton Gdns *SALV* BN13 ......28 A3
agton Hl *SALV* BN13 ....19 H5
agton Rd *SALV* BN13 ....27 H2
hire Dr *SALV* BN13 ....26 D4
tuary La *PUL/STOR* RH20 ...11 F4
field Av *LHPTN* BN17 ....23 E5
gate La *PUL/STOR* RH20 .....11 F2
own Av *ANG/EP* BN16 ....35 F4
own Cl *FERR* BN12 ....38 B3
ingham Ct
/SOMP * BN15 ....31 E4
ingham Ms
/BW BN14 ....29 E3
*/BN13 ....27 G2
ands *PUL/STOR* RH20 ....8 B3
wich Rd *WTHG* BN11 ....39 H4
La *LHPTN* BN5 ....9 F4
/STOR RH20 ....11 G3
Gdns *FERR* BN12 ....37 G3

Saxifrage Wy *SALV* BN13 ....26 D4
Saxon Cl *ANG/EP* BN16......36 C1
Saxon Rd *STEY/UB* BN44 .....15 E2
Saxony Rd *FIN/BW* BN14 .....28 D5
School Hl *FIN/BW* BN14 ....13 H5
PUL/STOR RH20 ....10 C3
School La *ARUN* BN18 ....21 F4
PUL/STOR RH20 ....10 B3
STEY/UB BN44 ....14 C2
School Rd *ARUN* BN18 ....12 C1
STEY/UB BN44 ....15 F3
Scotney Cl *SALV* BN13 ....27 E4
Sea Av *ANG/EP* BN16 ....35 G3
Sea Cl *FERR* BN12 ....38 D2
Seadown Pde
LAN/SOMP BN15 ....30 A4
Sea Dr *FERR* BN12 ....37 C4
Seafield Av *FERR* BN12 ....38 C4
Seafield Rd *ANG/EP* BN16...35 F5
Seahaven Gdns *SHOR* BN43...31 H4
Sea La *ANG/EP* BN16 ....35 E4
ANG/EP BN16 ....36 A4
ANG/EP BN16 ....37 E4
FERR BN12 ....38 B3
Sea Lane *ANG/EP* BN16 .....36 A3
FERR BN12 ....37 G2
Sea Lane Gdns *FERR* BN12...37 G3
Seamill Park Av *WTHG* BN11...41 F1
Seamill Park Crs *WTHG* BN11...41 F1
Seamill Wy *WTHG* BN11 ......41 E1
Sea Pl *FERR* BN12 ....38 D4
Sea Rd *ANG/EP* BN16 ....36 B3
LHPTN BN17 ....34 C5
Seaside Av *LAN/SOMP* BN15...31 E4
Seaside Cl *LAN/SOMP* BN15...31 E4
Seaside Rd *LAN/SOMP* BN15...31 E4
Seaton Cl *LHPTN* BN17 ....23 E5
Seaton La *LHPTN* BN17 ....23 E5
Seaton Pk *LHPTN* BN17 ....23 E5
Seaton Rd *LHPTN* BN17 ....23 E5
Seaview Av *ANG/EP* BN16 ...36 B4
ANG/EP BN16 ....37 E4
Seaview Ct *LAN/SOMP* BN15...30 C5
Seaview Rd *ANG/EP* BN16 ...36 A4
Sea View Rd *WTHG* BN11 .....2 A7
Seawaves Cl *ANG/EP* BN16...36 B3
Second Av *FIN/BW* BN14 .....29 E2
LAN/SOMP BN15 ....30 D2
Sedbury Rd *LAN/SOMP* BN15...30 B1
Sefton Cl *SALV* BN13 ....27 G3
Selborne Pl *LHPTN* * BN17...34 B4
Selborne Rd *LHPTN* BN17 ...34 B4
WTHG BN11 ....3 J2
Selborne Wy *ANG/EP* BN16...36 A3
Selden La *SALV* BN13 ....17 G5
WTHG BN11 ....3 J4
Selden Pde *SALV* * BN13 .....28 A2
Selden Rd *WTHG* BN11 ....3 J3
Selden's Ms *SALV* BN13 ......28 A3
Selden's Wy *SALV* BN13 .....28 A3
Selhurst Cl *ANG/EP* BN16 ...35 H3
Selkirk Cl *SALV* BN13 ....27 H5
Selsey Cl *SALV* BN13 ....28 A4
Selway Cl *LHPTN* BN17 ....34 C2
Selwyn Av *LHPTN* BN17 ....34 A1
Seventh Av *LAN/SOMP* BN15...30 D1
Shadwells Cl *LAN/SOMP* BN15...31 E2
Shadwells Rd *LAN/SOMP* BN15...31 E2
Shaftesbury Av *FERR* BN12...38 D1
Shaftesbury Rd *ANG/EP* BN16...35 F4
Shakespeare Rd *WTHG* BN11...2 B3
Shandon Gdns *FIN/BW* BN14...29 E3
Shandon Rd *FIN/BW* BN14 ...29 E3
Shandon Wy *FIN/BW* BN14...29 E3
Shannon Cl *ANG/EP* BN16 ...34 D4
Shardeloes Rd *ANG/EP* BN16...25 E3
Sheep Fold Av *ANG/EP* BN16...35 H2
Sheep Pen La *STEY/UB* BN44...14 C2
Shelby Rd *SALV* BN13 ....27 F3
Sheldon Ct *WTHG* * BN11 .....2 A6
Shelley Ldg *LHPTN* * BN17 ...34 C4
Shelley Rd *WTHG* BN11 ....2 C5
Shepherds Md *FIN/BW* BN14...20 B3
Sherbrooke Cl *SALV* BN13 ...27 G3
Sheridan Rd *FIN/BW* BN14 ...29 E4
Shermanbury Dr
PUL/STOR RH20 ....10 B2
Shermanbury Rd *FIN/BW* BN14...2 H1
Shetland Ct *SALV* BN13 ....27 E4
Shirley Cl *ANG/EP* BN16 .....35 G4
FIN/BW BN14 ....28 C2
Shirley Dr *FIN/BW* BN14 .....28 C2
Shooting Fld *STEY/UB* BN44...14 C1
Shopfield Cl *SALV* BN13 ....35 F2
Shopsdam Rd *LAN/SOMP* BN15...31 E5
Shoreham Rd *STEY/UB* BN44...15 G5
Short Furlong *LHPTN* BN17 ...34 C3
Silver Birch Dr *SALV* BN13 ...27 E4

Silverdale *WTHG* * BN11 .....41 E1
Silverdale Dr *LAN/SOMP* BN15...30 B4
Silver Gld *PUL/STOR* RH20 ...6 D3
Silver Wd *PUL/STOR* RH20 ...6 A2
Silver Wood Copse
PUL/STOR RH20 ....6 A2
Silverwood Ct *ANG/EP* * BN16...35 F3
Singleton Cl *FERR* BN12 .....37 G1
Singleton Crs *FERR* BN12 ...37 G1
Sir George's Pl *STEY/UB* BN44...14 B1
Skeyne Dr *PUL/STOR* * RH20...4 D4
Slindon Rd *FIN/BW* BN14 .....29 E3
Smallcroft Cl *LHPTN* BN17 ...33 H5
Smock Aly *PUL/STOR* RH20 ...6 D3
Smugglers Wk *FERR* BN12 ...38 D3
Snapes Rd *PUL/STOR* RH20...11 E1
Snowdrop Cl *ANG/EP* BN16...35 E1
Solent Cl *ANG/EP* BN16 ....34 D1
Solway Cl *LHPTN* BN17 ....34 C3
Somerset Cl *SALV* BN13 ....28 B4
Somerset Rd *ANG/EP* BN16...36 C2
FERR BN12 ....29 E4
Sompting Av *FIN/BW* BN14 ...29 F2
Sompting By-pass
FIN/BW BN14.............29 F2
FIN/BW BN14 ....29 H2
LAN/SOMP BN15 ....30 C3
Sopers *PUL/STOR* * RH20 .....4 D2
Sopers La *STEY/UB* BN44 .....14 C4
South Ash *STEY/UB* BN44 ....14 C4
South Av *FERR* BN12 ....38 D3
Southcourt Cl *ANG/EP* BN16...35 F2
Southcourt Rd *FIN/BW* BN14...2 D2
South Downs Wy *ARUN* BN18...12 C3
STEY/UB BN44 ....15 H5
Southdown Ter *STEY/UB* BN44...14 C2
Southdown View Cl
FIN/BW BN14.............29 G4
Southdown View Rd
FIN/BW BN14.............29 F4
Southdown View Wy
FIN/BW BN14.............29 F3
Southdown Wy *PUL/STOR* RH20...11 E1
South Dr *ANG/EP* BN16 ....35 C1
FERR BN12 ....37 F4
Southey Rd *WTHG* BN11 ....2 C6
South Farm Rd *FIN/BW* BN14...28 D3
Southfield Rd *FIN/BW* BN14...29 E4
Southfields Rd *LHPTN* BN17...34 C3
Southlands La *PUL/STOR* RH20...6 D2
South Ldg *LAN/SOMP* * BN15...30 B2
South Pas *LHPTN* BN17 ....34 C4
Southsea Av *FERR* BN12 .....38 D2
Southside *PUL/STOR* RH20 ...5 E4
South Strd *ANG/EP* BN16 .....36 B4
South St *LAN/SOMP* BN15 ...30 D5
SALV BN13 ....28 B5
WTHG BN11 ....3 F5
South Ter *LHPTN* BN17 ....34 C4
South Vw *ANG/EP* BN16 .....36 C4
Southview Dr *WTHG* BN11 ...39 F2
Southview Gdns *WTHG* BN11...39 E2
South View Ter *HFD* BN5 .....9 G4
Southwater Cl *FERR* BN12 ...38 A1
Southway *LHPTN* BN17 ....34 C4
Southways Av *FIN/BW* BN14...29 F3
Southwold Cl *SALV* BN13 .....19 H5
Sparks Cl *LHPTN* BN17 ....34 A3
Spear Hl *PUL/STOR* RH20 .....8 C1
Speedwell Cl *SALV* BN13 .....26 D4
Spencer Rd *LAN/SOMP* BN15...30 C4
Spey Cl *SALV* BN13 ....27 F1
Spierbridge Rd *PUL/STOR* RH20...10 B2
Spinnaker Cl *LHPTN* BN17 ...34 D3
The Spinney *ANG/EP* BN16...36 B4
PUL/STOR RH20 ....5 E4
Spinney La *PUL/STOR* RH20...6 B4
Spinney North *PUL/STOR* RH20...5 E4
Springfield Cl *ANG/EP* BN16...35 H3
Sproule Cl *ARUN* BN18 ....32 A2
Squadron Dr *SALV* BN13 .....27 E3
The Square *FIN/BW* BN14...29 E2
Squirrels Copse *PUL/STOR* RH20...11 H1
Stable La *FIN/BW* BN14 ....13 H5
Staffords Cl *ANG/EP* BN16 ...35 E3
Stag Cl *HFD* BN5 ....9 G2
Stane St *PUL/STOR* RH20 .....4 D2
Stane Street Cl *PUL/STOR* RH20...4 D2
Stanford Sq *WTHG* BN11 .....3 G5
Stanhope Rd *LHPTN* BN17 ...34 B2
WTHG BN11 ....3 G5
Stanley Rd *LHPTN* BN17 ....34 A1
WTHG BN11 ....3 F2
Stansfield Ct *LHPTN* BN17 ...35 G2
Staples Barn *HFD* BN5 ....9 F3
Staples Barn La *HFD* BN5 ....9 F3
Station Pde *ANG/EP* * BN16...35 H2
LAN/SOMP * BN15 ....30 D4

WTHG * BN11 ....39 F1
Station Rd *ANG/EP* BN16 .....25 E5
ANG/EP BN16 ....35 G2
ANG/EP BN16 ....36 A2
HFD BN5.............9 F3
PUL/STOR RH20 ....4 B4
STEY/UB BN44 ....14 D2
WTHG BN11 ....3 F2
Stean Furlong *LHPTN* BN17...33 H1
Steep Cl *FIN/BW* BN14.............19 H1
Steepdown Rd *LAN/SOMP* BN15...30 B1
Steep La *FIN/BW* BN14 ....19 H1
Steeple Vw *SALV* BN13 ....28 B4
Sterling Pde *ANG/EP* * BN16...35 F3
Sternway *LHPTN* BN17 ....34 D3
Stewards Ri *ARUN* BN18 .....21 E5
The Steyne *WTHG* BN11 .....3 G5
Steyne Gdns *WTHG* BN11 .....3 G5
Steyning By-Pass
STEY/UB BN44.............15 E4
Steyning Cl *LHPTN* BN17 .....38 A1
LAN/SOMP BN15 ....30 C1
Steyning Crs *PUL/STOR* RH20...10 B2
Stipenhoke *HFD* * BN5 ....9 H4
Stoke Abbott Rd *WTHG* BN11...2 E4
Stone Cl *SALV* BN13 ....28 A3
Stonefields *ANG/EP* BN16 ...35 F3
Stonehurst Rd *SALV* BN13 ...28 A4
Stone La *SALV* BN13 ....28 A3
Stopham Cl *FIN/BW* BN14 ...28 B4
Stor Meadow *PUL/STOR* RH20...10 C2
Storrington Ri *FIN/BW* BN14...20 A2
Storrington Rd *PUL/STOR* RH20...7 F4
Stour Cl *SALV* BN13 ....27 F1
Stour Rd *SALV* BN13 ....27 F1
The Strand *FERR* BN12 .....37 F4
FERR BN12 ....38 A1
Strand Pde *FERR* * BN12 .....27 H5
Strathmore Cl *SALV* BN13 ...27 H5
Strathmore Rd *SALV* BN13 ...27 H5
Strawberry La *PUL/STOR* RH20...7 G5
The Street *ANG/EP* BN16 ...35 F3
ANG/EP BN16 ....36 A2
LAN/SOMP BN15 ....30 D1
PUL/STOR RH20 ....5 H2
PUL/STOR RH20 ....7 G4
SALV BN13 ....18 A4
STEY/UB BN44 ....15 E3
Stuart Cl *WTHG* BN11 ....3 K1
Sugden Rd *WTHG* BN11 ....3 J2
Sullington Copse
PUL/STOR RH20 ....10 D2
Sullington Gdns *FIN/BW* BN14...20 A2
Sullington La *PUL/STOR* RH20...11 E4
Summerdown Cl *SALV* BN13...27 E4
Summerfields *FIN/BW* BN14...13 H5
Summerlea Cl *ANG/EP* BN16...35 E1
Summerlea Gdns *LHPTN* * BN17...34 B3
Sunderland Ms *ANG/EP* * BN16...35 G3
Sunflower Cl *ANG/EP* BN16...23 H5
Sunningdale Ct *FERR* * BN12...38 B1
Sunningdale Rd *SALV* BN13...27 G3
Sunny Cl *FERR* BN12 ....38 D3
Sunset La *PUL/STOR* RH20 ...6 B4
Surrey St *ARUN* BN18 ....21 F4
LHPTN BN17 ....34 A4
WTHG BN11 ....2 D6
Surrey Whf *ARUN* BN18 ....21 G4
Sussex Gdns *ANG/EP* BN16...35 E2
Sussex Rd *LAN/SOMP* BN15...31 H4
WTHG BN11 ....3 F3
Sussex St *LHPTN* BN17 ....34 C4
Sutherland Cl *ANG/EP* BN16...35 E4
Sutton Av *ANG/EP* BN16 .....35 F4
Swallows Cl *LAN/SOMP* BN15...31 H4
The Swallows *LHPTN* * BN17...34 C4
Swallows Green Dr *SALV* BN13...27 F4
Swanbourne Cl
LAN/SOMP BN15 ....31 E1
Swanbourne Rd *LHPTN* BN17...34 A1
Swan Cl *PUL/STOR* RH20.......10 B2
Swan Ct *PUL/STOR* * RH20 ...4 C4
Swan Vw *PUL/STOR* RH20 ...4 D4
Swift Wy *LHPTN* BN17 ....22 D5
Swillage La *ANG/EP* BN16....17 F3
Sycamore Cl *ANG/EP* BN16...25 E5
Sylvan Rd *LAN/SOMP* BN15...30 A3

T

Talbot Rd *LHPTN* BN17 ....33 H3
Tamar Av *SALV* BN13 ....27 F1
Tamar Cl *SALV* BN13 ....27 F2
Tamarisk Wy *ANG/EP* BN16...35 H4
FERR BN12 ....37 G4
Tansy Md *PUL/STOR* RH20 ...10 A2

Tanyard La *STEY/UB* BN44 ....**14** B2
Tarrant Sq *ARUN* * BN18 ....**21** G3
Tarrant St *ARUN* BN18 ....**21** G4
Tarrant Whf *ARUN* BN18 ....**21** G4
Tarring Ga *SALV* * BN13 ....**28** B5
Tarring Rd *WTHG* BN11 ....**2** A2
Tasman Cl *ANG/EP* BN16 ....**35** C4
Tasman Wy *SALV* BN13 ....**27** F2
Tavy Cl *SALV* BN13 ....**27** F3
Tavy Rd *SALV* BN13 ....**27** F3
Taw Cl *SALV* BN13 ....**27** G2
Telgarth Rd *FERR* BN12 ....**37** F4
The Templars *FIN/BW* BN14 ....**29** F2
Ten Acres *WTHG* BN11 ....**40** D1
Tennyson Av *ANG/EP* BN16 ....**34** D3
Tennyson Rd *WTHG* BN11 ....**2** D4
Terminus Pl *LHPTN* BN17 ....**34** A3
Terminus Rd *LHPTN* BN17 ....**33** H3
The Terrace *FERR* * BN12 ....**38** B2
................*LAN/SOMP* BN15 ....**30** D5
Terringes Av *SALV* BN13 ....**27** H4
Test Rd *LAN/SOMP* BN15 ....**30** A3
Teville Ga *WTHG* BN11 ....**2** E2
Teville Pl *WTHG* BN11 ....**2** D2
Teville Rd *WTHG* BN11 ....**2** D2
Thackeray Rd *FIN/BW* BN14 ....**29** G5
Thakeham Cl *ANG/EP* BN16 ....**36** C1
................*FERR* BN12 ....**37** H2
Thakeham Copse
................*PUL/STOR* RH20 ....**11** G2
Thakeham Dr *FERR* BN12 ....**37** H2
Thakeham Rd *PUL/STOR* RH20 ....**11** E2
Thalassa Rd *WTHG* BN11 ....**41** E1
Thames Cl *LHPTN* BN17 ....**34** D4
Thames Wy *SALV* BN13 ....**27** G2
The Thatch Ct
................*LAN/SOMP* * BN15 ....**31** E1
The Thatchway *ANG/EP* BN16 ....**24** D4
................*ANG/EP* BN16 ....**35** C4
Thatchway Cl *LHPTN* BN17 ....**34** A2
Thesiger Cl *WTHG* BN11 ....**29** H5
Thesiger Rd *WTHG* BN11 ....**29** H5
Third Av *LAN/SOMP* BN15 ....**30** D2
Thirlmere Crs *FIN/BW* BN14 ....**30** A4
Thomson Cl *SALV* BN13 ....**27** E3
Thorgate Rd *LHPTN* BN17 ....**33** G1
Thorncroft Rd *LHPTN* BN17 ....**34** B2
Thorn Rd *WTHG* BN11 ....**2** C6
Thornscroft *STEY/UB* BN44 ....**14** C1
Threals Copse *PUL/STOR* RH20 ....**6** D4
Threal's La *PUL/STOR* RH20 ....**6** D3
Thurlow Rd *WTHG* BN11 ....**3** H2
Tideway *ANG/EP* BN16 ....**34** C4
Timber Cl *SALV* BN13 ....**27** F4
Timberlands *PUL/STOR* RH20 ....**10** C3
Timberlea Cl *PUL/STOR* RH20 ....**6** B3
Timberleys *LHPTN* BN17 ....**34** C1
Tithe Gn *ANG/EP* BN16 ....**35** E3
Titnore La *SALV* BN13 ....**26** C2
Titnore Wy *FERR* BN12 ....**26** D4
Toddington La *LHPTN* BN17 ....**23** E5
Toddington Pk *LHPTN* BN17 ....**23** F5
Toronto Cl *SALV* BN13 ....**27** G3
Torridge Cl *SALV* BN13 ....**27** F2
Torton Hill Rd *ARUN* BN18 ....**21** E5
Tower Rd *LAN/SOMP* BN15 ....**30** C4
................*WTHG* BN11 ....**3** G3
Towers Rd *STEY/UB* BN44 ....**15** G3
Town Quay *ARUN* * BN18 ....**21** G3
Townsend Crs *LHPTN* BN17 ....**34** C2
Treharne Cl *SALV* BN13 ....**27** G2
Trent Cl *LAN/SOMP* BN15 ....**30** B3
Trent Rd *WTHG* BN11 ....**38** D2
Treveor Cl *WTHG* BN11 ....**2** D4
Trinity Wy *LHPTN* BN17 ....**34** C4
Tristram Cl *LAN/SOMP* BN15 ....**29** H2
True Blue Prec *LHPTN* BN17 ....**34** A1
Truleigh Rd *STEY/UB* BN44 ....**15** G3
Truro Ct *WTHG* * BN11 ....**39** F3
Tudor Cl *FIN/BW* BN14 ....**13** H5
................*PUL/STOR* RH20 ....**5** G5
Tudor Dr *STEY/UB* BN44 ....**15** F2
Tudor Village *PUL/STOR* RH20 ....**11** H1
Tunsgate *STEY/UB* BN44 ....**14** C2
Turner Rd *FIN/BW* BN14 ....**29** F3
Turners Md *PUL/STOR* RH20 ....**10** A2
Turnpike Rd *ARUN* BN18 ....**12** D2
Turnpike Wy *PUL/STOR* RH20 ....**8** C4
Twittenside *STEY/UB* * BN44 ....**15** G4
Twitten Wy *SALV* BN13 ....**28** B5
Twyford Cl *SALV* BN13 ....**27** H3
Twyford Gdns *SALV* BN13 ....**27** H3
Twyford Rd *SALV* BN13 ....**27** H3
Tyne Cl *SALV* BN13 ....**27** F2
The Tynings *LAN/SOMP* BN15 ....**30** D4

U

Ullswater Dr *ANG/EP* BN16 ....**34** D1
Ullswater Rd *LAN/SOMP* BN15 ....**30** A4
Undermill Rd *STEY/UB* BN44 ....**15** G3
Union Pl *WTHG* BN11 ....**3** F4
Uplands Av *SALV* BN13 ....**20** A5
Upper Boundstone La
................*LAN/SOMP* BN15 ....**30** C2
Upper Brighton Rd
................*FIN/BW* BN14 ....**28** D3
Upper Dr *ANG/EP* BN16 ....**36** C4
Upper High St *WTHG* BN11 ....**3** G2
Upper Station Rd *HFD* BN5 ....**9** F3
Upper West Dr *FERR* BN12 ....**37** F3
Upper West La *LAN/SOMP* BN15 ....**30** D2
Upton Gdns *SALV* BN13 ....**28** A5
Upton Rd *SALV* BN13 ....**28** A5

V

Vale Av *FIN/BW* BN14 ....**20** A4
Vale Dr *FIN/BW* BN14 ....**20** A4
Valencia Rd *WTHG* BN11 ....**39** F1
Valentine Cl *FIN/BW* BN14 ....**28** C2
Vale Wk *FIN/BW* BN14 ....**20** A4
Valley Rd *LAN/SOMP* BN15 ....**30** B1
Vancouver Cl *SALV* BN13 ....**27** G3
Vancouver Rd *SALV* BN13 ....**27** F3
Varey Rd *SALV* BN13 ....**27** E3
Veras Wk *PUL/STOR* RH20 ....**11** H3
Vermont Dr *ANG/EP* BN16 ....**36** B3
Vermont Rd *ANG/EP* BN16 ....**36** B3
Vernon Cl *ANG/EP* BN16 ....**35** F3
Veronica Cl *ANG/EP* BN16 ....**36** B4
Vicarage Flds *SALV* BN13 ....**27** G2
Vicarage La *FIN/BW* BN14 ....**36** A3
................*STEY/UB* BN44 ....**14** C2
Victoria Gdns *LHPTN* * BN17 ....**34** A4
Victoria Park Gdns *WTHG* BN11 ....**2** C3
Victoria Rd *WTHG* BN11 ....**2** D3
Vincent Cl *LAN/SOMP* BN15 ....**30** C3
Vineries Cl *SALV* BN13 ....**28** B3
Viney Cl *PUL/STOR* RH20 ....**8** B3

W

Wadhurst Dr *FERR* BN12 ....**38** A2
Wakehurst Pl *ANG/EP* BN16 ....**35** F2
Walders Rd *ANG/EP* BN16 ....**34** D2
Wallace Av *WTHG* BN11 ....**39** E2
Wallace Ms *WTHG* * BN11 ....**39** E3
Wallace Pde *WTHG* * BN11 ....**39** E2
Wallace Rd *ANG/EP* BN16 ....**35** F2
Walnut Av *ANG/EP* BN16 ....**35** E3
Walnut Ldg *FIN/BW* * BN14 ....**2** C1
Walnut Tree Wy *SALV* BN13 ....**27** E4
Walpole Av *FERR* BN12 ....**38** C2
Walters Gn *LHPTN* * BN17 ....**23** E4
Walton Cl *SALV* BN13 ....**28** A3
Walton Ldg *SALV* BN13 ....**28** A3
Wantley Hill Est *HFD* BN5 ....**9** H4
Wantley La *PUL/STOR* RH20 ....**10** D2
Wantley Rd *FIN/BW* BN14 ....**20** B5
Warminghurst Cl
................*PUL/STOR* RH20 ....**8** B3
Warner Rd *FIN/BW* BN14 ....**29** G5
Warnham Cl *FERR* BN12 ....**38** C3
Warnham Ms *FERR* * BN12 ....**38** D3
Warnham Rd *FERR* BN12 ....**38** C2
The Warren *FERR* BN12 ....**37** G4
Warren Crs *ANG/EP* BN16 ....**36** A2
Warren Cft *PUL/STOR* RH20 ....**10** A3
Warren Gdns *FIN/BW* BN14 ....**28** C2
Warren Rd *FIN/BW* BN14 ....**28** C2
Warwick Gdns *WTHG* BN11 ....**3** G5
Warwick La *WTHG* * BN11 ....**3** G5
Warwick Pl *WTHG* BN11 ....**3** H4
Warwick Rd *WTHG* BN11 ....**3** H5
Warwick St *WTHG* BN11 ....**3** F5
Washington Rd
................*PUL/STOR* RH20 ....**10** D3
Water La *ANG/EP* BN16 ....**25** F3
................*LHPTN* BN17 ....**34** A2
................*PUL/STOR* RH20 ....**10** D1
Waters Edge *PUL/STOR* RH20 ....**4** B5
Watersfield Rd *FIN/BW* BN14 ....**28** C4
The Waterside *LHPTN* * BN17 ....**33** H3
Waverley Rd *ANG/EP* BN16 ....**35** F3

Wavertree Rd *FERR* BN12 ....**38** C1
Wayside *LAN/SOMP* * BN15 ....**30** B4
Wayside Av *SALV* BN13 ....**27** G2
The Way *ANG/EP* BN16 ....**36** B4
Wear Cl *SALV* BN13 ....**27** F2
Wear Rd *SALV* BN13 ....**27** F2
Weavers Hl *ANG/EP* BN16 ....**25** F4
Weavers Ring *ANG/EP* BN16 ....**25** F4
Welland Cl *SALV* BN13 ....**27** G1
Welland Rd *SALV* BN13 ....**27** G1
Wellesley Av *FERR* BN12 ....**37** G1
Well House Rd *PUL/STOR* * RH20 ....**8** C3
Wellingham La *SALV* BN13 ....**19** H5
Wells Ct *WTHG* * BN11 ....**39** F3
Wembley Av *LAN/SOMP* BN15 ....**30** C3
Wembley Gdns
................*LAN/SOMP* BN15 ....**30** C3
Wenban Rd *WTHG* BN11 ....**2** E3
Wenceling Cottages
................*LAN/SOMP* BN15 ....**31** H4
Wendy Rdg *ANG/EP* BN16 ....**35** E2
Wentworth Cl *SALV* BN13 ....**28** A1
Wentworth Ct *ANG/EP* * BN16 ....**36** B3
................*LAN/SOMP* BN15 ....**31** F4
................*WTHG* BN11 ....**39** F2
West Beach Pk South
................*LHPTN* * BN17 ....**33** H4
West Beach Rd
................*LAN/SOMP* BN15 ....**31** H4
Westbourne Av *FIN/BW* BN14 ....**2** E4
Westbrooke *WTHG* BN11 ....**2** E4
West Buildings *WTHG* BN11 ....**2** D6
West Chiltington Rd
................*PUL/STOR* RH20 ....**5** G5
................*PUL/STOR* RH20 ....**6** C5
Westcourt Pl *FIN/BW* BN14 ....**2** D1
Westcourt Rd *FIN/BW* BN14 ....**2** D2
Westdean Rd *FIN/BW* BN14 ....**28** C4
West Dr *ANG/EP* BN16 ....**24** C5
................*FERR* BN12 ....**37** F4
West End La *HFD* BN5 ....**9** G3
West End Wy *LAN/SOMP* BN15 ....**30** C5
Westergate Cl *FERR* BN12 ....**37** G2
Western Cl *LAN/SOMP* BN15 ....**30** B5
Western Ldg *LAN/SOMP* * BN15 ....**30** B2
Western Pl *WTHG* BN11 ....**2** D6
Western Rd *LAN/SOMP* BN15 ....**30** B5
................*LHPTN* BN17 ....**34** B4
Western Rd North
................*LAN/SOMP* BN15 ....**30** B5
Western Rw *WTHG* BN11 ....**2** D6
Western Ter *FIN/BW* * BN14 ....**29** G2
Westfield Rd *ANG/EP* BN16 ....**36** B4
West Head *LHPTN* BN17 ....**34** C4
West Hl *SALV* BN13 ....**19** H4
West Hill Cl *SALV* * BN13 ....**19** H4
Westlake Cl *SALV* BN13 ....**28** A4
Westland Av *FIN/BW* BN14 ....**28** B5
Westlands *ANG/EP* BN16 ....**34** D2
................*FERR* BN12 ....**37** F3
West La *LAN/SOMP* BN15 ....**30** D3
West Mare La *PUL/STOR* RH20 ....**5** F5
West Md *ANG/EP* BN16 ....**35** H3
West Onslow Cl *FERR* * BN12 ....**37** F1
West Pde *WTHG* BN11 ....**39** E4
Westpark La *FERR* BN12 ....**38** D2
West Preston Ms
................*ANG/EP* * BN16 ....**35** H3
West Ridings *ANG/EP* BN16 ....**35** H4
West St *LAN/SOMP* BN15 ....**30** A2
................*PUL/STOR* RH20 ....**10** B3
................*WTHG* BN11 ....**2** D6
West Tyne *SALV* BN13 ....**27** G4
Westview Ter *FIN/BW* BN14 ....**13** H5
Westward La *PUL/STOR* RH20 ....**6** B3
West Wy *LAN/SOMP* BN15 ....**31** H4
................*LHPTN* BN17 ....**19** H1
................*SALV* BN13 ....**19** G5
Wharf Rd *LHPTN* BN17 ....**33** H3
Wheatcroft *LHPTN* BN17 ....**34** A2
Wheel Wrights Cl *ARUN* BN18 ....**21** H1
Whitebeam Rd *SALV* BN13 ....**27** F4
White Horses Wy *ANG/EP* BN16 ....**34** D3
Whitelea Rd *LHPTN* BN17 ....**34** A2
White Styles Rd
................*LAN/SOMP* BN15 ....**30** A2
Whiteways Cl *LHPTN* BN17 ....**34** A2
Whylands Av *SALV* BN13 ....**27** G1
Whylands Cl *SALV* BN13 ....**27** G1
Whylands Crs *SALV* BN13 ....**27** G1
Wick Farm Rd *LHPTN* BN17 ....**33** H2
Wick St *LHPTN* BN17 ....**34** A1
Widewater Cl *LAN/SOMP* BN15 ....**31** H4
Wigmore Rd *FIN/BW* BN14 ....**29** E3

Willard Wy *PUL/STOR* RH20 ....**3**
Willow Av *ANG/EP* BN16 ....**3**
Willow Brook *LHPTN* BN17 ....**3**
Willowbrook Rd *FIN/BW* BN14 ....**3**
Willow Cl *LAN/SOMP* BN15 ....**3**
................*PUL/STOR* RH20 ....**3**
................*STEY/UB* BN44 ....**3**
Willow Ct *WTHG* BN11 ....**3**
Willow Crs *SALV* BN13 ....**3**
Willowhayne Av *ANG/EP* BN16 ....**3**
Willowhayne Cl *ANG/EP* BN16 ....**3**
Willowhayne Crs *ANG/EP* BN16 ....**3**
The Willows *ANG/EP* BN16 ....**3**
................*FIN/BW* * BN14 ....**3**
................*LAN/SOMP* * BN15 ....**3**
................*PUL/STOR* RH20 ....**3**
................*PUL/STOR* * RH20 ....**1**
Willow Wy *PUL/STOR* RH20 ....**3**
Wills Cl *ARUN* BN18 ....**3**
Wilson Ct *ARUN* BN18 ....**3**
Wilton Cl *ANG/EP* BN16 ....**3**
Wilton Dr *ANG/EP* BN16 ....**3**
Winchelsea Gdns *WTHG* BN11 ....**3**
Winchester Rd *ANG/EP* BN16 ....**3**
................*WTHG* BN11 ....**3**
Windermere Ct *FERR* * BN12 ....**3**
Windermere Crs *FERR* BN12 ....**2**
Windlesham Gdns
................*ANG/EP* BN16 ....**3**
Windmill Cl *PUL/STOR* RH20 ....**3**
................*STEY/UB* BN44 ....**3**
Windmill Copse *PUL/STOR* RH20 ....**0**
Windmill Dr *ANG/EP* BN16 ....**3**
Windmill La *HFD* BN5 ....**3**
Windmill Rd *LHPTN* BN17 ....**1**
Windrush Cl *SALV* BN13 ....**2**
Windsor Cl *ANG/EP* BN16 ....**3**
Windsor Dr *ANG/EP* BN16 ....**3**
Windsor Rd *WTHG* BN11 ....**3**
Windsor Wy *LAN/SOMP* BN15 ....**3**
Windward Cl *LHPTN* BN17 ....**3**
Winston Av *LAN/SOMP* BN15 ....**3**
Winterbourne Cl *SALV* BN13 ....**3**
Winterbourne Wy *SALV* BN13 ....**3**
The Winter Knoll *LHPTN* BN17 ....**3**
Winterton Ldg *LHPTN* * BN17 ....**3**
Winton Pl *WTHG* BN11 ....**3**
Wisborough La *PUL/STOR* RH20 ....**1**
Wiston Av *FIN/BW* BN14 ....**3**
Wiston Cl *FIN/BW* BN14 ....**2**
Withdean Av *FERR* BN12 ....**3**
Woelfs Cl *PUL/STOR* * RH20 ....
Wolstenbury Rd *ANG/EP* BN16 ....**3**
Woodard Rd *LAN/SOMP* BN15 ....**3**
Woodbridge Pk *ANG/EP* BN16 ....**3**
Woodcote La *LHPTN* BN17 ....**2**
Woodland Av *SALV* BN13 ....**1**
Woodlands Av *ANG/EP* BN16 ....**3**
Woodlands Cl *ANG/EP* BN16 ....**2**
................*SALV* BN13 ....**3**
Woodlands Rd *LHPTN* BN17 ....**3**
Woodlea Rd *SALV* BN13 ....**3**
Woodmancote Rd
................*FIN/BW* BN14 ....**2**
Woodpecker La *PUL/STOR* RH20 ....**1**
Woodpecker Wy *SALV* BN13 ....**2**
Woodside Cl *PUL/STOR* RH20 ....
Woodside Rd *FIN/BW* BN14 ....
Woods Wy *FERR* BN12 ....**3**
Wood Vw *ARUN* BN18 ....**3**
Wooldridge Wk *LHPTN* BN17 ....**3**
Woolvens Rw *HFD* * BN5 ....
Worcester Ct *WTHG* * BN11 ....**3**
Wordsworth Rd *WTHG* BN11 ....**3**
Worthing Rd *LHPTN* BN17 ....**3**
Wren Cl *PUL/STOR* * RH20 ....
Wychwood Gdns *WTHG* BN11 ....**3**
Wyke Av *WTHG* BN11 ....**3**
Wykeham Cl *STEY/UB* BN44 ....**1**
Wykeham Rd *WTHG* BN11 ....**3**
Wyndham Lea *PUL/STOR* RH20 ....**3**

Y

Yeoman Rd *SALV* BN13 ....**2**
Yeoman Wy *SALV* BN13 ....**2**
York Gdns *LHPTN* BN17 ....**3**
York Rd *LHPTN* BN17 ....**3**
................*WTHG* BN11 ....**3**

rley CE First School
UN BN18 .... 12 C1

rley Museum
UN BN18 .... 12 B4

rley Railway
UN BN18 .... 12 B3

Bowling
HG BN11 .... 2 E6

ering School
C/EP BN16 .... 36 A1

ena Swimming Pool
HG BN11 .... 3 J5

ore School
HG BN11 .... 2 E4

dale Preparatory School
L/STOR RH20 .... 5 E4

del Castle
UN BN18 .... 21 G3

del & District Hospital
UN BN18 .... 21 F3

del FC
UN BN18 .... 21 H3

del Toy & Military Museum
UN BN18 .... 21 H3

Fitzalan Swimming Pool
UN BN18 .... 21 H4

Yacht Club
PTN BN17 .... 34 A4

gton CE Primary School
L/STOR RH20 .... 8 B3

n Health Centre
C/EP BN16 .... 35 G2

ber Castle
EY/UB BN44 .... 15 E3

ber Road First School
/BW BN14 .... 29 F3

lwater &
orthing Cemetery
WTHG BN11 .... 28 D4

lwater CE F & M School
WTHG BN11 .... 28 D4

lwater Industrial Estate
/BW BN14 .... 29 G3

lwater Manor School
/BW BN14 .... 29 E4

lands Trading Estate
/BW BN14 .... 2 B2

side Industrial Estate
C/EP BN16 .... 35 F1

ctonbury Leisure Centre
L/STOR RH20 .... 10 A2

ry Industrial Estate
L/STOR RH20 .... 10 D4

wood Middle School
HG BN11 .... 3 H1

ury Ring
/BW BN14 .... 20 C1

am & Patching CE Primary
hool
LV BN13 .... 18 B5

aught Theatre & Cinema
HG BN11 .... 3 F4

eld School
PTN BN17 .... 34 B1

on CE Secondary
hool for Girls
HG BN11 .... 3 K2

n Trading Estate
/BW BN14 .... 29 G4

Cinema
HG BN11 .... 3 G6

lands Business Park
/BW BN14 .... 29 F1

sbrook CP School
/BW BN14 .... 29 F4

sbrook Middle School
/BW BN14 .... 29 F4

sbrook Trading Estate
/BW BN14 .... 29 F3

gton Health Centre
LV BN13 .... 27 G3

gton High School
LV BN13 .... 27 H4

gton Primary School
LV BN13 .... 27 H2

Preston CP School
C/EP BN16 .... 36 B2

street Medical Centre
PTN BN17 .... 34 A3

Worthing Industrial Estate
/BW BN14 .... 29 G4

rove County First School
HG BN11 .... 39 E1

rove County
ants School
PTN BN17 .... 34 B2

English Bowling Association
WTHG BN11 .... 3 H4

English Martyrs RC
Primary School
FERR BN12 .... 27 G4

Environment Agency
WTHG BN11 .... 3 F5

Ferring CE Primary School
FERR BN12 .... 37 G2

Ferring FC
FERR BN12 .... 37 F2

Field Place First School
FERR BN12 .... 27 G5

Flora Mcdonald County
Junior School
WTHG BN11 .... 33 H2

Ford Airfield Industrial Estate
ARUN BN18 .... 32 A1

Freshbrook County First School
LAN/SOMP BN15 .... 30 D3

Friends of Arundel Castle
Cricket Club
ARUN BN18 .... 21 F2

Funpark
LHPTN BN17 .... 34 A5

Garcia Trading Estate
SALV BN13 .... 39 E1

Georgian Gardens CP School
ANG/EP BN16 .... 35 H2

Gerrard House Business Centre
ANG/EP BN16 .... 36 A2

Gerston Business Park
PUL/STOR RH20 .... 10 B4

Goring by Sea CE First School
FERR BN12 .... 38 B2
FIN/BW BN14 .... 29 E2

Goring Cricket Club
FERR BN12 .... 37 H2

Guildbourne Shopping Centre
WTHG BN11 .... 3 G5

Ham Bridge Trading Estate
FIN/BW BN14 .... 29 H5

Ham Manor Golf Club
ANG/EP BN16 .... 24 C5

Harbour Park
LHPTN BN17 .... 34 A5

The Hawthorns First School
SALV BN13 .... 27 F4

Hazelwood Trading Estate
FIN/BW BN14 .... 29 F4

Heene CE First School
WTHG BN11 .... 2 C3

Heene Community Centre
WTHG BN11 .... 2 B5

Henfield & District
Leisure Centre
HFD BN5 .... 9 G2

Highdown Hill
FERR BN12 .... 26 B4

Highdown Special School
SALV BN13 .... 27 H4

Hill Barn Municipal Golf Club
WTHG BN11 .... 28 D1

The John Horniman School
WTHG BN11 .... 3 H4

Lancing Business Centre
LAN/SOMP BN15 .... 30 B4

Lancing Health Centre
LAN/SOMP BN15 .... 30 D3

The Laurels County First School
SALV BN13 .... 27 E3

Lineside Industrial Estate
LHPTN BN17 .... 33 G2

Littlehampton
Community School
LHPTN BN17 .... 34 B2

Littlehampton Golf Club
LHPTN BN17 .... 33 H4

Littlehampton Health Centre
LHPTN BN17 .... 34 B3

Littlehampton Hospital
LHPTN BN17 .... 34 B3

Littlehampton Museum
LHPTN BN17 .... 34 B3

Littlehampton Swimming Centre
LHPTN BN17 .... 34 C5

Littlehampton Town FC
LHPTN BN17 .... 34 C3

Lyminster County Infant School
LHPTN BN17 .... 34 A1

Lyndhurst First School
WTHG BN11 .... 3 K2

Manor Sports Ground Pavilion
FIN/BW BN14 .... 29 E4

Marlborough Business Centre
LAN/SOMP BN15 .... 30 B5

Martlets Trading Estate
FERR BN12 .... 38 B1

Meadow Road Industrial Estate
WTHG BN11 .... 30 A5

Modern Mould Business Centre
LHPTN BN17 .... 33 G2

Modern Moulds Business Centre
WTHG BN11 .... 30 B5

Montague Shopping Centre
WTHG BN11 .... 3 F4

The Museum
STEY/UB BN44 .... 14 C2

Northbrook College
FIN/BW BN14 .... 28 D4
SALV BN13 .... 27 E5
WTHG BN11 .... 3 F4

Northbrook Trading Estate
FIN/BW BN14 .... 29 F3

North Lancing First &
Middle School
LAN/SOMP BN15 .... 30 D1

Oaklands Business Centre
ANG/EP BN16 .... 39 E1

Old Darlington Mushroom Farm
Industrial Estate
ANG/EP BN16 .... 25 F4

The Orchards Community
Middle School
FERR BN12 .... 27 G5

Our Lady of Sion Junior School
WTHG BN11 .... 2 E4

Our Lady of Sion School
WTHG BN11 .... 2 D5

Palatine School
FERR BN12 .... 27 G4

Parkland Business Centre
LAN/SOMP BN15 .... 30 C5

Pavilion Theatre
WTHG BN11 .... 3 F6

Piggott's Business Park
WTHG BN11 .... 2 D3

Queen Alexandra
Hospital Home
WTHG BN11 .... 2 B5

RC Cemetery
ARUN BN18 .... 21 F3

Riverside Industrial Estate
LHPTN BN17 .... 33 G3

Rudford Industrial Estate
ARUN BN18 .... 32 C2

Rustington Community
Primary School
ANG/EP BN16 .... 35 E2

Rustington Retail Park
ANG/EP BN16 .... 35 G1

Rustington Trading Estate
ANG/EP BN16 .... 35 F1

The Rydon Community School
PUL/STOR RH20 .... 11 E2

St Catherines RC School
LHPTN BN17 .... 34 A2

St John Baptist Primary School
FIN/BW BN14 .... 13 G5

St Margarets Primary School
ANG/EP BN16 .... 25 E2

St Marys CE Primary School
LHPTN BN17 .... 32 D4
PUL/STOR RH20 .... 4 D3

St Marys RC Primary School
WTHG BN11 .... 2 C4

St Peters CE Primary School
HFD BN5 .... 9 F2

St Philips RC Primary School
ARUN BN18 .... 21 F3

St Wilfrids RC Primary School
ANG/EP BN16 .... 25 E3

Sandhurst School
WTHG BN11 .... 3 J4

Shoreham Airport
SHOR BN43 .... 31 H2

Springfield First School
FIN/BW BN14 .... 29 F5

Station Approach
Industrial Estate
PUL/STOR RH20 .... 4 B4

Steyning Athletic Club
STEY/UB BN44 .... 14 B2

Steyning Grammar School
STEY/UB BN44 .... 14 C1

Steyning Health Centre
STEY/UB BN44 .... 14 C2

Steyning St Andrews CE
Primary School
STEY/UB BN44 .... 14 C1

Steyning Sports Centre
STEY/UB BN44 .... 14 B1

Steyning Town FC
STEY/UB BN44 .... 14 C1

Storrington First School
PUL/STOR RH20 .... 10 B2

Storrington Lawn Tennis Club
PUL/STOR RH20 .... 10 B3

Summerlea Community
Primary School
ANG/EP BN16 .... 35 E1

Sussex Clinic
WTHG BN11 .... 2 C5

Swandean Hospital
SALV BN13 .... 27 G1

Templars County
Infants School
LAN/SOMP BN15 .... 30 A3

Thakeham First School
PUL/STOR RH20 .... 7 G2

Thomas A Becket First School
SALV BN13 .... 28 B4

Thomas A Becket Middle School
FIN/BW BN14 .... 28 C4

Thornberry Middle School
LAN/SOMP BN15 .... 31 E4

Timberlaine Trading Estate
FIN/BW BN14 .... 29 G4

Town Hall Museum &
Art Gallery
WTHG BN11 .... 3 F4

Upper Beeding Primary School
STEY/UB BN44 .... 15 F3

Vale CP School
SALV BN13 .... 20 A4

Vinalls Business Centre
HFD BN5 .... 9 G4

Water Lane Industrial Estate
PUL/STOR RH20 .... 11 E1

Watersmead Business Park
LHPTN BN17 .... 22 D5

West Bank Fort
LHPTN BN17 .... 34 A5

Westholme Clinic
FERR BN12 .... 38 C2
WTHG BN11 .... 2 C5

West Park CE Controlled School
FERR BN12 .... 38 C2

West Sussex School of English
STEY/UB BN44 .... 14 C2

White Rose Touring Park
LHPTN BN17 .... 23 E4

Whitestyles Middle School
LAN/SOMP BN15 .... 30 A3

Whytemead First School
FIN/BW BN14 .... 29 F4

Wickbourne Infant School
LHPTN BN17 .... 33 H2

Wick FC
LHPTN BN17 .... 23 F5

Wigmore AFC
FIN/BW BN14 .... 29 E2

Wigmore Trading Estate
FIN/BW BN14 .... 29 G4

Windmill Theatre & Cinema
LHPTN BN17 .... 34 A5

Winston Business Centre
LAN/SOMP BN15 .... 30 B4

Worthing Athletics Track
WTHG BN11 .... 38 D1

Worthing Crematorium
FIN/BW BN14 .... 13 F3

Worthing & District
Magistrates Court
WTHG BN11 .... 2 D4

Worthing FC
FIN/BW BN14 .... 2 B1

Worthing Golf Club
FIN/BW BN14 .... 20 C5

Worthing High School
FIN/BW BN14 .... 28 D5

Worthing Hospital
WTHG BN11 .... 3 G2

Worthing Pier
WTHG BN11 .... 3 G6

Worthing Priority Care
NHS Trust
ANG/EP BN16 .... 35 G3

Worthing RFC
ANG/EP BN16 .... 25 G5

Worthing Sixth Form College
SALV BN13 .... 38 D1

WWT Arundel
ARUN BN18 .... 21 H1